Monet.

N B SINCLAIR

CHARTWELL BOOKS, INC.

Published by
CHARTWELL BOOKS, INC.
A Division of BOOK SALES, INC.
110 Enterprise Avenue
Secaucus, New Jersey 07094

Produced by
Brompton Books Corp.
15 Sherwood Place
Greenwich, CT 06830

ISBN 1-55521-762-1

Printed in Hong Kong

LIST OF PLATES

CLAUDE MONET

1840–1926

The paintings of Claude Monet are the most popular in the Western world. No artist's work is more widely disseminated, through public collections and exhibitions as well as in reproduction in posters, postcards, and more arcane media. Such widespread exposure can have a strong effect of dislocation on a work of art in depriving it of a context; the best example of this phenomenon is Leonardo da Vinci's *Mona Lisa*, a painting where the very lack of contextual information is a part of most viewers' response to and understanding of the painting and its putative aura of mystery. The accessibility of impressionist painting, of which Monet's work is the best-known, owes much to the fact that it requires no knowledge of its context in order to understand it in terms of the artists' expressed intentions. In that one of Monet's expressed intentions was to capture, objectively, fleeting impressions of light and color, to the extent to which he was successful in his aims we should be able to respond to his painting without any knowledge of its context. Of course it is naive to suggest that any work of art can be purely objective; if that were the case the work of one photographer would be indistinguishable from that of another and photography would not be an art form. With painting this is even more true as the artist has to make the same choices in terms of composition and subject as a photographer as well as a whole host of others such as the medium and how he manipulates it. Nonetheless, although there are a variety of interpretations which can be made of impressionist painting, as with all art, perhaps with impressionism we can come closer to the eye of the artist than with any other painting.

Claude Oscar Monet was born in Paris in November 1840 but moved with his family to the Channel port of Le Havre around 1846. His father was a partner in a family grocery business and, although he expected his son to join him in this, did not oppose his decision to follow an artistic career. Perhaps young Monet's success in saving 2000 francs from selling caricatures of local worthies persuaded his father that he had a saleable talent. More important to Monet's artistic development were the two years he spent under the supervision of Eugène Boudin. Boudin's choice of commonplace subject matter in his seascapes of the region around Le Havre, the immediacy of his vision and his habit of painting in the open air (this was, contrary to popular belief, not a practice invented by the Impressionists) all deeply impressed the young Monet.

Exposure to Boudin's art perhaps influenced Monet's choice of training when he arrived in Paris in May 1859. His father expected Monet to seek acceptance as a pupil of Thomas Couture and entrance to the Ecole des Beaux-Arts. Couture was a classical academic artist and a model of the success an artist could enjoy if he followed the conventional path through training at the Ecole and exhibition at the Salon, the official state art exhibition held biennially. Monet, however, preferred to register at the Académie Suisse; not only was this cheap but also the students received only sporadic and informal tuition.

Boudin's influence may perhaps also be seen in the artistic circles in which Monet moved in Paris. Monet reported approvingly on the work of the Barbizon painters when he visited the Salon of 1859. Barbizon is a village in the forest of Fontainebleau, south of Paris, and the painters who worked there included Millet, Rousseau, Corot, Daubigny, and Jongkind. Like Boudin they preferred unidealized landscapes as their subjects and painted them in close-toned earth colors and grays. This understated Romanticism contrasts strongly with the large-scale heroic work of Romantics such as Delacroix.

A more radical and urban group of artists who also attracted Monet were those to be found in the Brasserie des Martyrs, congregating around Gustave Courbet. Although they used such Romantic devices of Delacroix as a heroic celebration of the human figure, Courbet's circle termed themselves Realists for their determined acceptance of modern, urban subject matter anathema to Romantics of any complexion. There was a strong element of social commentary in some Realist art but others regarded depicting the lower classes as an autonomous artistic activity, unconnected with a search for social improvement. Monet, although he held vaguely left-wing views all his life, seems to have belonged to the latter group.

Monet's earliest work in Paris shows little influence of his new acquaintances. *Corner of a Studio* (1861) is richly painted and expertly composed but Realist as much in the manner of 17th-century Dutch art or Chardin as of Courbet. Before he could experiment further Monet was unlucky enough to be picked by lottery for national service in the army. He spent a year in North Africa before falling ill with dysentery and allowing his father to obtain his discharge.

It was only after his return to Paris in 1862 that Monet began to develop as a landscape painter. He registered this time at the studio of Charles Gleyre. Although a former pupil of the archetypal Neoclassicist David, Gleyre ran his studio on similarly informal lines to the Académie Suisse and did not impose rigid tuition for the Ecole des Beaux-Arts entrance examination on pupils such as Monet who preferred to develop their own interests. In Gleyre's studio Monet made some friends who were to be important for the development of French art in the late nineteenth century. They included Pierre-Auguste Renoir, Alfred Sisley, and Frédéric Bazille, all around Monet's age. Together these young artists spent Easter 1863 at Barbizon, meeting the artists they admired and painting together *sur le motif*. Monet's work from this time, such as *The Road from Chailly to Fontainebleau* (1865), is still very much in the tradition of Corot and Millet, and seascapes such as *La Pointe de la Hève at Low Tide* (1864-65) remind us of Boudin and Jongkind, and although his paintings began as oil sketches done on the spot, much reworking and finishing took place in the studio.

The year 1863 was of great importance to these young artists of the future avant-garde. For the first time a major alternative to the Salon was organized, the Salon des Refusés, the aim of which was to show all 4000 of the works rejected by the hanging committee of the official Salon. This gave the first major public exposure to painting outside the convention of large-scale classical painting which had become so much a part of the public face of French cultural life through the Salon and the Ecole des Beaux-Arts. A major feature of the Salon des Refusés was Edouard Manet's *Le Déjeuner sur l'Herbe*. This painting caused such a stir because it showed a picnic scene in which two of the participants were naked or scantily clad young women. While the naked female form was of central importance to classical-derived imagery of the official Salon painters, it was unacceptable to adopt it in what was essentially a contemporary scene. Realism was bad enough in itself, but to subvert classical painting by incorporating one of its chief motifs in a realist or naturalist painting was too much for the Salon committee.

Manet's work greatly attracted Monet and other young painters in search of a new kind of painting. They saw in it a means to depicting everyday life, both urban and rural, without the Romanticism of Realists such as Courbet, and using new pictorial means. Manet's use of novel spatial conventions such as flattened perspective, close-up or 'cut-off' elements in his art was influenced by his study of Japanese prints then becoming popular in artistic circles in France. His use of dramatic tonal contrasts which eliminated half-tones was, furthermore, partly influenced by photography. The thoroughness of Manet's search for a truly new kind of art, and *Le Déjeuner sur l'Herbe* in particular, inspired Monet to begin work in 1865 on a huge canvas with the same title. Monet had already had some success in having two seascapes accepted for the 1865 Salon. His aspirations in painting *Le Déjeuner sur l'Herbe* were less complex than Manet's had been: he sought principally to create a painting of uncompromisingly contemporary subject matter on a scale large enough to lend it the monumentality and gravitas of more conventional Salon paintings. The subject was a picnic scene in the forest near Chailly with the figures of his friends painted life size. The painting was damaged by damp and later cut down in size, but the composition is known from a large oil study now in the Pushkin Museum, Moscow.

Despite Monet's modest success at the 1865 Salon, the late 1860s were lean years for him. His father had cut off his allowance, partly because Monet refused to marry his mistress Camille Doncieux who gave birth to his son Jean in 1867. He became adept at borrowing money from wealthy friends such as Bazille and in 1868 a portrait commission, *Madame Gaudibert* (1868), from a wealthy family enabled him to set up home at Etretat on the Channel coast. Paris as a subject interested Monet, as can be seen in such works as *Boulevard des Capucines* (1873). He was, however, never a true Parisian in inclination like Degas or Manet. Portrait and interior scenes still dominated his work at this period and the influence of Manet in his composition, handling of paint, and coloration is still very evident in works such as *Camille (the Green Dress)* (1866).

The year 1867 brought about something of a revolution in Monet's approach to painting, for it was to this year that he dated his adoption of a truly impressionist technique. The term 'impressionist' is not a precise term in any sense and was used very freely in the late 19th century to describe almost any painting of the avant garde which did not belong to the classical school. Even as applied to the artists who exhibited at the great Impressionist exhibitions of 1874-86, or to them as individuals, it is imprecise. Monet's work of 1867 to 1926, when he died, can all be described as 'impressionist,' yet his art underwent several transformations both in vision and technique. But the common factor with all Monet's impressionist works is an attempt to capture nature as it appears at any given moment and to infuse each painting with the artist's particular sensations in the face of nature. One concomitant of this view was that for landscape painting to be truly impressionist it had to be painted from start to finish in the open air, and should be abandoned when light effects changed. The series paintings of the 1890s, especially the *Grainstacks* and *Rouen Cathedral*, were the logical result of this approach. To render correctly the effects of light came to mean for Monet painting purely in color, not in tone. In his earliest impressionist works such as *Bathers at La Grenouillère* (1869) Monet still used black pigment for shadowed areas. Soon, however, he banished pure black as it is not a constituent of any color of light; shadow was to be rendered in combinations of color, as can be seen in *Hôtel des Roches Noires at Trouville* (1870), not in washes of black or brown as had been the practice for centuries. In seeking in *Bathers at La Grenouillère* to capture the complexities of light on water, reflected light, shadow, light through foliage and so on, Monet, and Renoir who painted the same scene with him, had not abandoned their search for a new subject as well as a new technique or a new vision in art. La Grenouillère was a bathing place on the river Seine frequented by the middle and lower-middle classes of both sexes. As such it was an appropriate and typical, if slightly risqué, contemporary subject for an artist with Monet's interests.

In July 1870 war broke out between France and Prussia and rather than be called up for army service Monet fled with his family to London. It was a sensible decision; his friend Bazille was to be killed in the war. This visit was important for Monet's art as it introduced him to a city that was to be his most constant urban subject; over the years Monet painted more than a hundred views of the Palace of Westminster, such as *London, Houses of Parliament* (1905), and the Thames bridges. The interest lay for him, perhaps, in the subtlety of the light effects to be found in London, whose smoky atmosphere rendered even sunny days hazy. While in London Monet consorted with other refugees such as Pissarro and Daubigny, visiting public galleries and exhibitions with the former. It was probably Daubigny who made the lastingly important introduction of Monet to the dealer Paul Durand-Ruel who showed a Monet seascape in his Bond Street gallery in January 1871.

Durand-Ruel was to be Monet's dealer until the dealer's death in 1923. He was responsible for Monet's rise in fortune in the early 1870s after he returned to settle with his family at the small Seineside town of Argenteuil, six miles from Paris. By 1873 Durand-Ruel had bought paintings to the value of nearly 30,000 francs. Monet, it seems, still managed to live beyond his means, keeping himself and Camille, to whom he was now married, in the style to which they had been accustomed all their lives. Argenteuil was the perfect setting for Monet to develop, practice and continue to formulate his art. Although until recently completely rural in setting, and still retaining a rural aspect to its north bank, suburban sprawl was beginning to reach the Seine at Argenteuil in the 1870s. Thus Monet could choose rural harmony or social gathering as his subject and with either he would have the complexities of light provided by the river. It was also the first time he made and painted a garden, an activity that was to dominate his last twenty years.

By this time the various circles of avant-garde painters and writers had long been debating the desirability of organizing an alternative exhibition to the Salon to exhibit a varied selection of modern painting. The success of the Salon des Refusés of 1863 and of Manet's one-man show at the 1867 World Fair was encouraging, particularly to artists such as Cézanne and Pissarro who had been consistently unsuccessful in submitting to the Salon. Others such as Bazille had strongly believed on principle that an alternative show should be held, while others such as Manet believed that only by taking the fight to the enemy camp, that is by exhibiting new art at the Salon, would any progress be made. Monet's position seems always to have been pragmatic. He would continue to submit to the Salon but would also support an alternative exhibition, probably as it represented a further vehicle for promoting his art.

In December 1873 fifteen painters including Monet, Renoir, and Pissarro signed a charter setting up a limited company to exhibit their work. The exhibition was held at a studio in the boulevard des Capucines formerly occupied by the photographer Nadar. Monet exhibited five oil paintings, including a Thames view called *Impression: Sunrise* (1872) which led to a hostile critic coining the term 'Impressionists.' The show was certainly not a complete failure and attracted a considerable number of visitors. Monet was able to sell *Impression: Sunrise* for 800 francs after this, and at later Impressionist exhibitions in 1876 and 1879 many of the works he exhibited were listed as already sold. This gives an interesting insight into Monet's marketing of his art at this period. By exhibiting a high proportion of sold works he no doubt hoped to create an aura of desirability around his work thus attracting more sales and higher prices.

Monet's paintings of the mid- and late-1870s suggest that his pictorial interests were beginning to dominate any concerns he might once have shared with the Realists or the Naturalists of introducing a social critique or commentary into his art. Although his wife and son feature often in his scenes of his garden at Argenteuil they form just another element in the composition, further vehicles for his pursuit of authentic light effects and truth to nature. Even where Monet is painting pure landscape, though, his vision is perhaps not as coldly implacable as he would have us believe. His paintings around Argenteuil suggest a rural idyll that is not borne out by contemporary descriptions of encroaching industry and untreated sewage fouling the Seine. Only rarely does Monet allow such concerns to impinge on his vision as in *Railway Bridge at Argenteuil* (1874). A major exception to this rejection of industrialization, although one that would not be repeated, is the series of eight views of the Gare Saint Lazare in Paris which Monet exhibited as a group at the 1877 Impressionist exhibition. But even here what has caught Monet's attention are the extraordinarily complex and fugitive effects of light in the reflexions in the glass station roof and the billowing smoke and steam. Thus it seems it was the challenge of the subject's visual effects which caught Monet's attention and not an interest in progress through industrialization or, conversely, the condition of modern urban humanity. Indeed the figures in the painting are indistinguishable as individuals; they are reduced, as one critic was to put it, to a 'clamor.'

Although success was increasingly Monet's as the 1870s progressed he was not above adopting new types of subject matter when his main dealer, Durand-Ruel, suggested it. The market almost certainly explains Monet's ventures into still life in the early 1880s. None the less he succeeded in suggesting new pictorial possibilities in the way fruit, flowers, and so on are strewn apparently haphazardly across a surface in a way quite different from his earlier restrained Chardinesque efforts. It was a line of development he did not follow through properly, however, for another thirty years or so.

The 1880s are often seen as a period of crisis for Impressionism. Whatever the variations among the various artists who exhibited at the Impressionist exhibitions, and the variety within each artist's work, Impressionism was in danger of becoming an 'idiot eye.' Cézanne's comment on Monet that 'he is an eye but my God, what an eye' expresses well the limitations that a contemporary found in his approach. For an artist such as Cézanne the way forward lay in structure, both the literal structuring of his paintings' surfaces and in finding and expressing the essential structures of his subjects. For a younger artist such as Georges Seurat, who had never been an Impressionist, the answer lay in scientific rules for picture-making with paint applied in dots of pure color according to laws governing the relationships of colors, and with the lines of the composition arranged according to their supposedly objective emotive qualities. Monet abhorred such an impersonal approach to art but it is ironic that in some of his seascapes of 1886-90 Seurat, with his laborious studio-based technique, succeeded in capturing, in a much more objective way than Monet, the fleeting effects of light and reflexion.

Monet's response to the crisis was to seek out more complex and extreme natural effects, whether Norwegian snowscapes or the harsh glowing color of the French Mediterranean coast. He also began to experiment unashamedly with the composition of his landscapes. Whereas before he would tinker with parts of the composition, eliminating minor elements which he found compromised the harmony of the composition, now he experimented with whole compositions. Unlike Manet, Monet rarely introduced overtly Japanese motifs into his paintings, but his approach in the 1880s is strongly influenced by Japanese landscape print designers such as Hokusai and Hiroshige. This can be seen in the way that the tilted-up foreground mass of cliff in several works such as *Cliff at Dieppe* (1882) catapults us straight into the flat, perspectiveless background of sea and sky. The application of paint is also quite different, both from the rather smooth, creamy surface of the early 1860s' paintings and from the tight-packed, strokes of unbroken color of, for example, *Bathers at La Grenouillère*. Now the brushstrokes are much more loose and vibrant, varying from coiling to straight within a single painting. Increasingly, also, Monet seems consciously to be seeking a dynamic and harmony of color within his paintings which are unrelated to his response to the motif. Moreover where linear perspective has been banished as an organizational device, color seems to replace it in defining, if not conventional recession, then a sense of depth in the painting as in *Ravine of the Creuse* (1889).

Monet did not entirely give up figure painting during this time. During the late 1870s he and Camille and their children had set up home with one of his patrons, Ernest Hoschedé and his wife Alice, who had fallen on hard times. Monet and Alice had formed an attachment and after Camille's premature death in 1879 they set up home together. They finally married in 1891, after Ernest Hoschedé's death. This complex and varied domestic life provided Monet with two women and a large number of children to people his garden- and river-scenes. As with the works of the 1870s, however, there is an element of detachment in his treatment of the figures who meld disconcertingly with the landscape to become just another element of nature.

The early 1890s brought one of the great revolutions in Monet's art, the series paintings, chief among which were the *Grainstacks* (1891), and the *Rouen Cathedral* series (1892-94). Each series purports to represent the same subject under the varying light conditions that prevail at various times of day and in different types of weather. In the rigor of the approach and to the extent that, for all their supposedly objective recording of natural effects, their color and composition are highly artificial, the series paintings have been seen as a riposte to Seurat and a departure from Monet's former Impressionist practice. And yet for all that, they can also be seen as a linear and logical development of Impressionism. The decision repeatedly to paint the same subject can be seen as an attempt by Monet to transcend the subject to find some 'pure' sensation of nature and natural effects.

This view seems to be confirmed by the way Monet developed his art in the last thirty years of his life. In 1890 he bought the freehold of his home at Giverny and proceeded to create a garden. This incorporated a Japanese-inspired lily pond on which he was increasingly to focus as a subject for his paintings. Indeed apart from a group of paintings of London of 1904 and a further series of Venice of 1912 Monet never again ventured beyond his garden in his art. In veneration of his new motif Monet seems almost to have begun his artistic development again in exploring it. The earliest views such as *The Japanese Bridge* are quite conventionally composed with tonal contrast and surface facture which harks back to the late 1860s. In the series of 48 works exhibited in 1909 called 'A Series of Water Landscapes' his view has drifted down from the bridge toward the surface of the water. The paint has become more dilute but the forms of the lilypads and the reflected images are still distinct. In later years the vision of leaves, lilypads, clouds and sky begins to dissolve as Monet's view descends still further toward the surface of the water; no longer can we know whether we see surface reflexions or a view upward from the surface.

Monet's work in his old age is a tremendous triumph of hope, and a transcendence of his wife's death in 1911 and his son Jean's in 1914. At the suggestion of his friend the politician Georges Clemenceau Monet arranged to leave his 1914-16 waterlily paintings to the French nation. He extended the idea by painting several enormously long canvases which came to be arranged in two circular rooms in the Orangerie of the Tuileries in Paris. They have been described as the 'Sistine Chapel of Impressionism' and represented for Monet a celebration of post-First World War peace. They can also be seen as the ultimate expression of those Impressionist ideals that Monet had been exploring for sixty years.

TRAIN IN THE COUNTRY, 1870
Oil on canvas, 19¾×25½in (50×65cm)
Musée d'Orsay, Paris

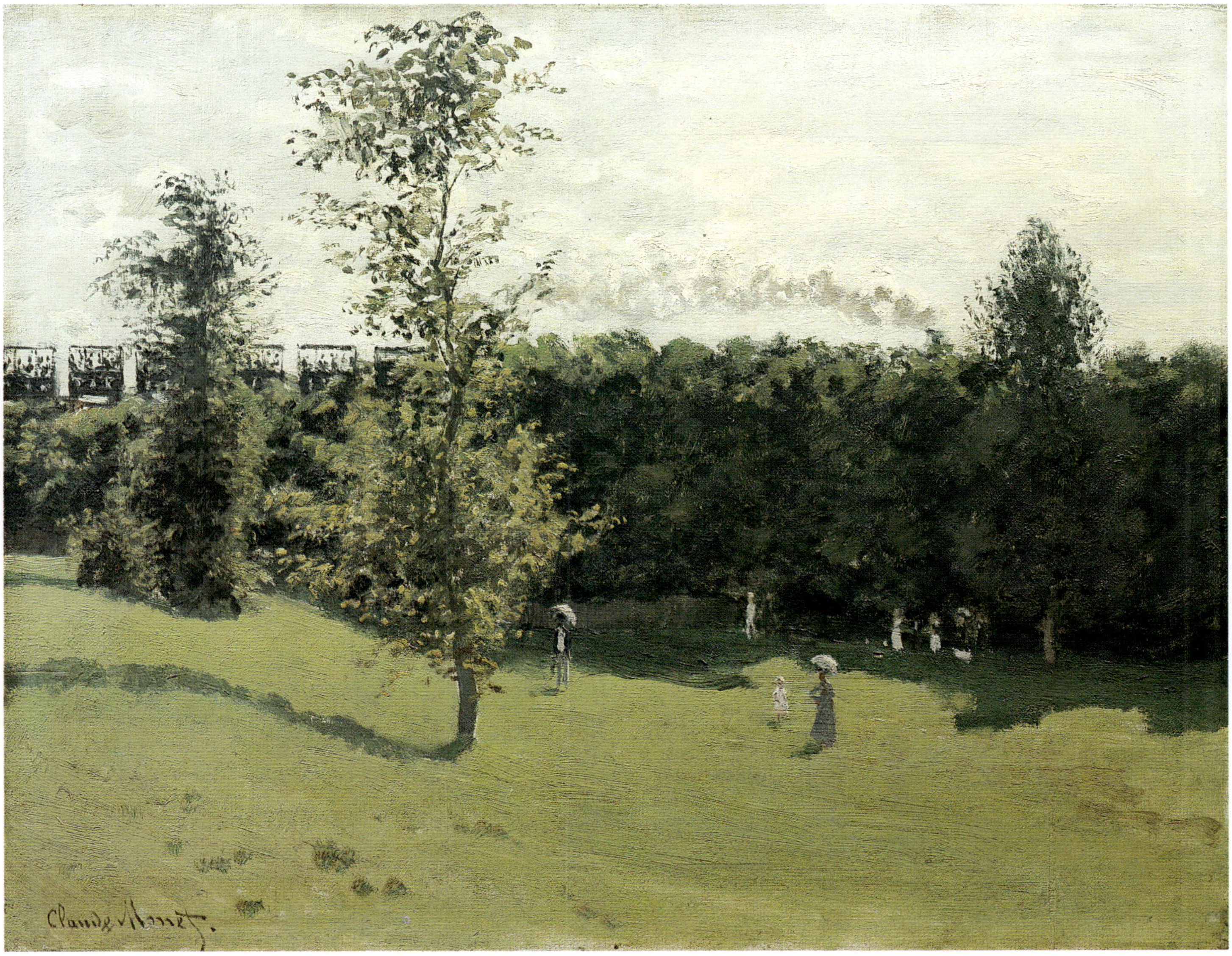

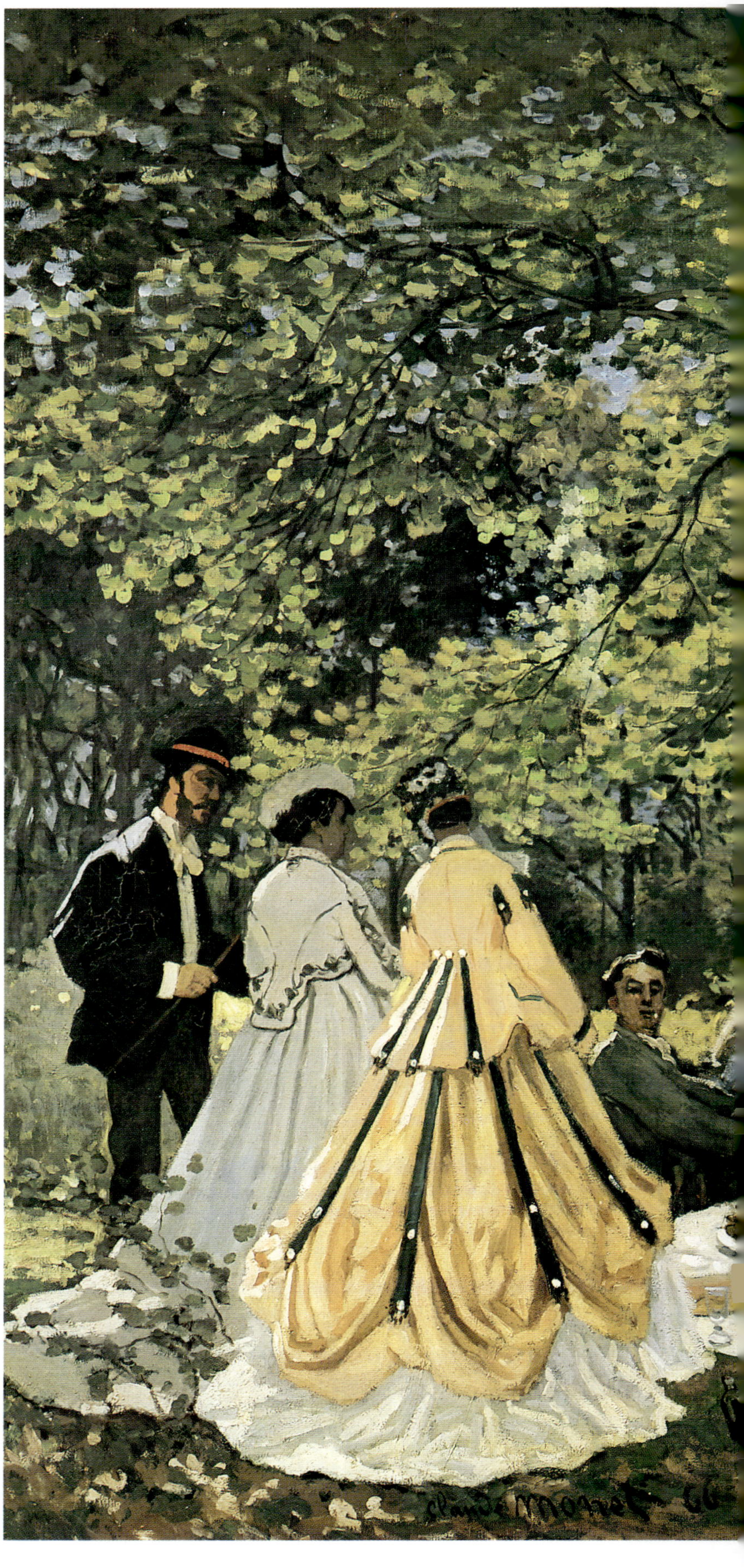

Le Déjeuner sur l'Herbe (final study), 1865 (dated 1866)
Oil on canvas, 51¼×71¼in (130×181cm)
Puskhin Museum, Moscow

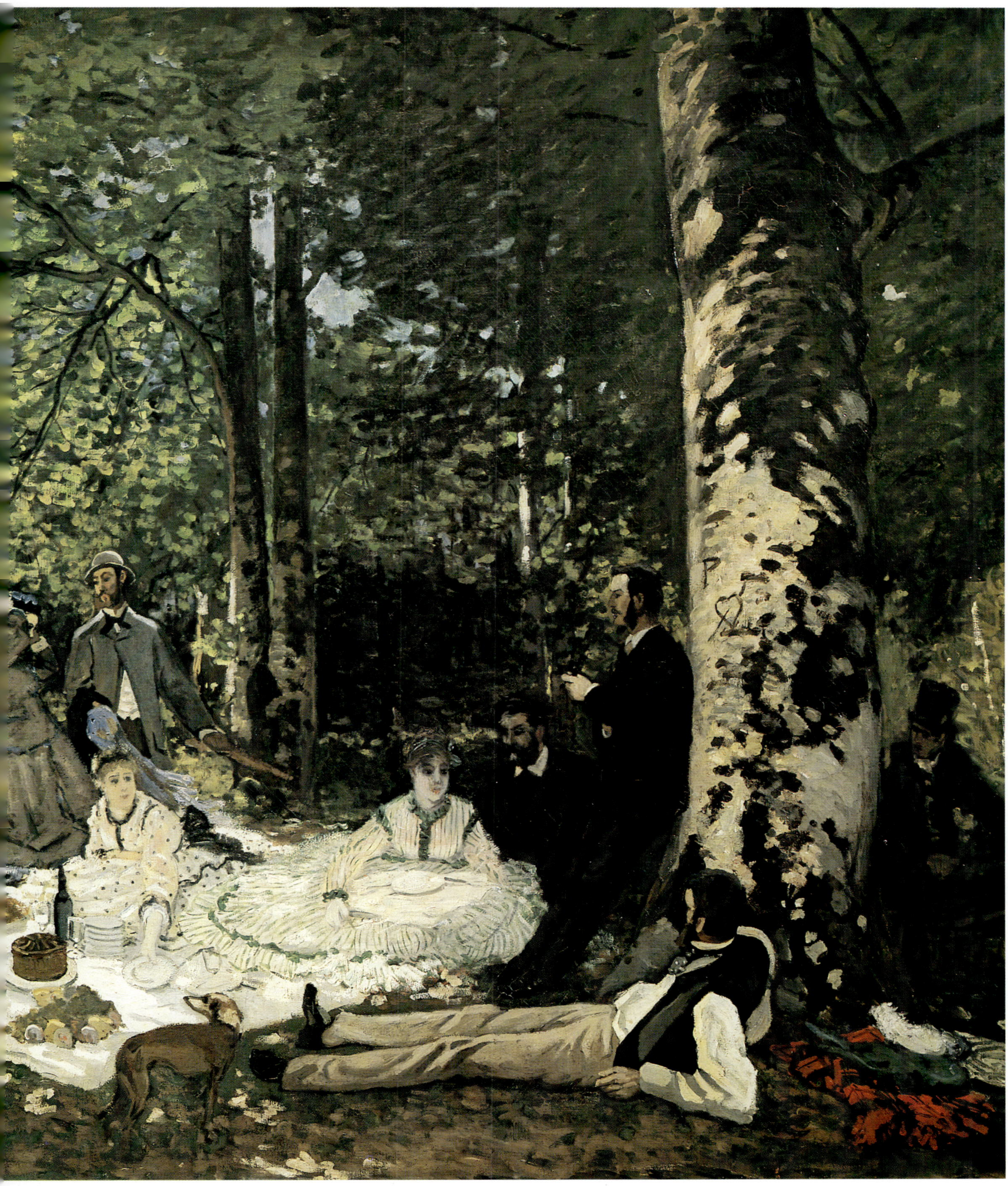

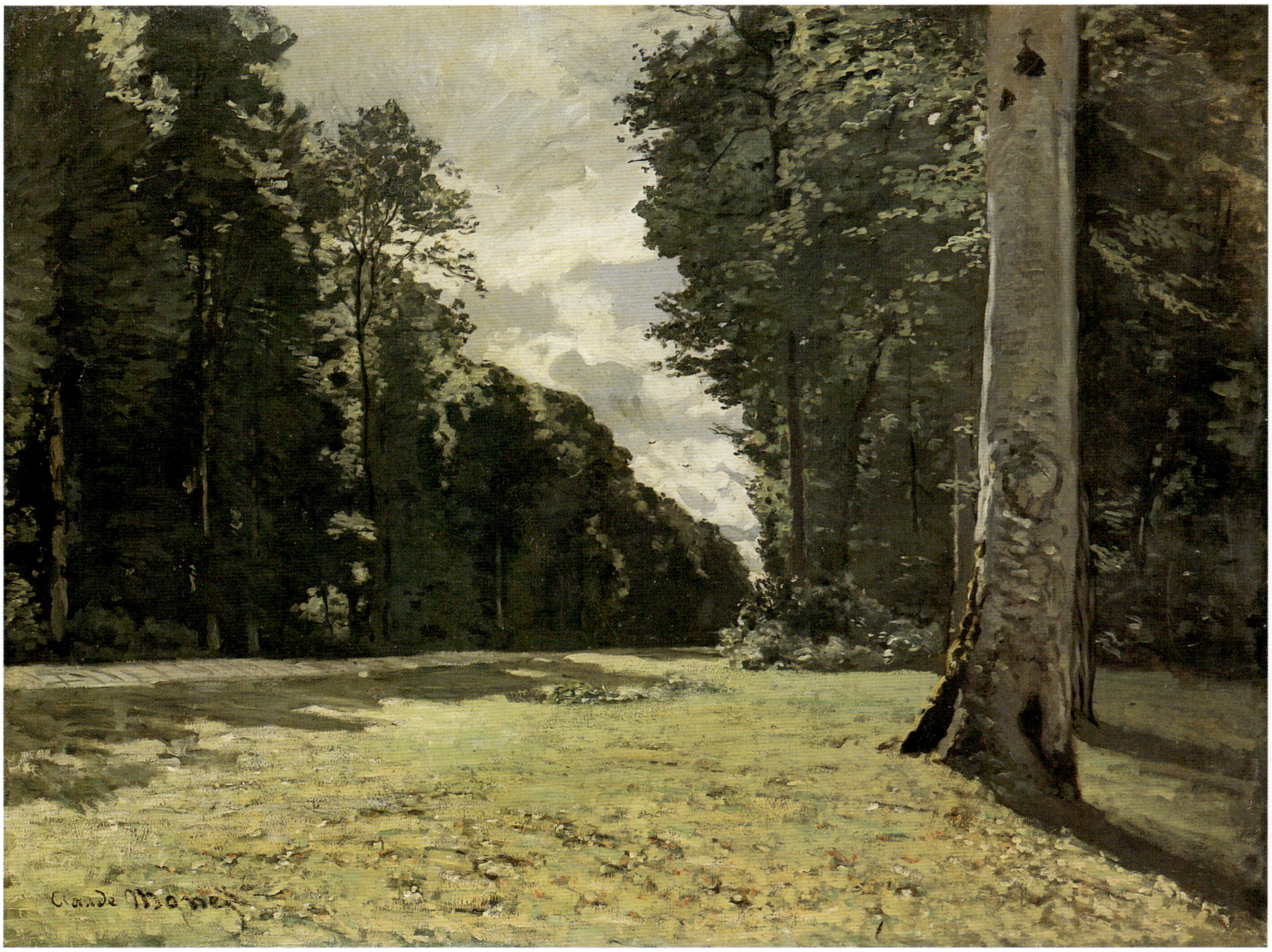

The Road from Chailly to Fontainebleau, 1865
Oil on canvas, 38¼×51¼ (97×130cm)
The Ordrupgaard Collection, Copenhagen

La Pointe de la Hève at Low Tide, 1864-65
Oil on canvas, 35½×59¼in (90.2×150.5cm)
Kimbell Art Museum, Fort Worth, Texas

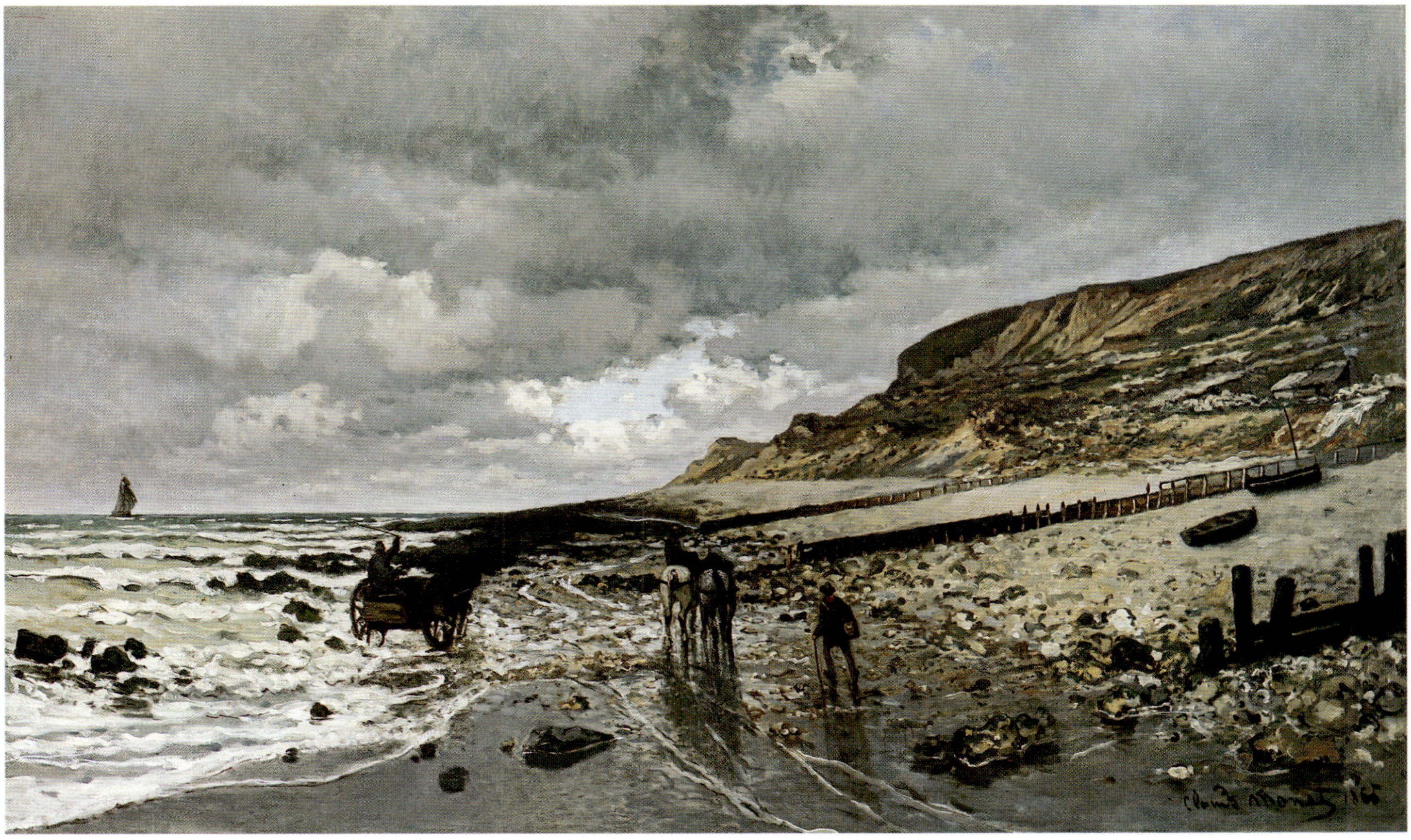

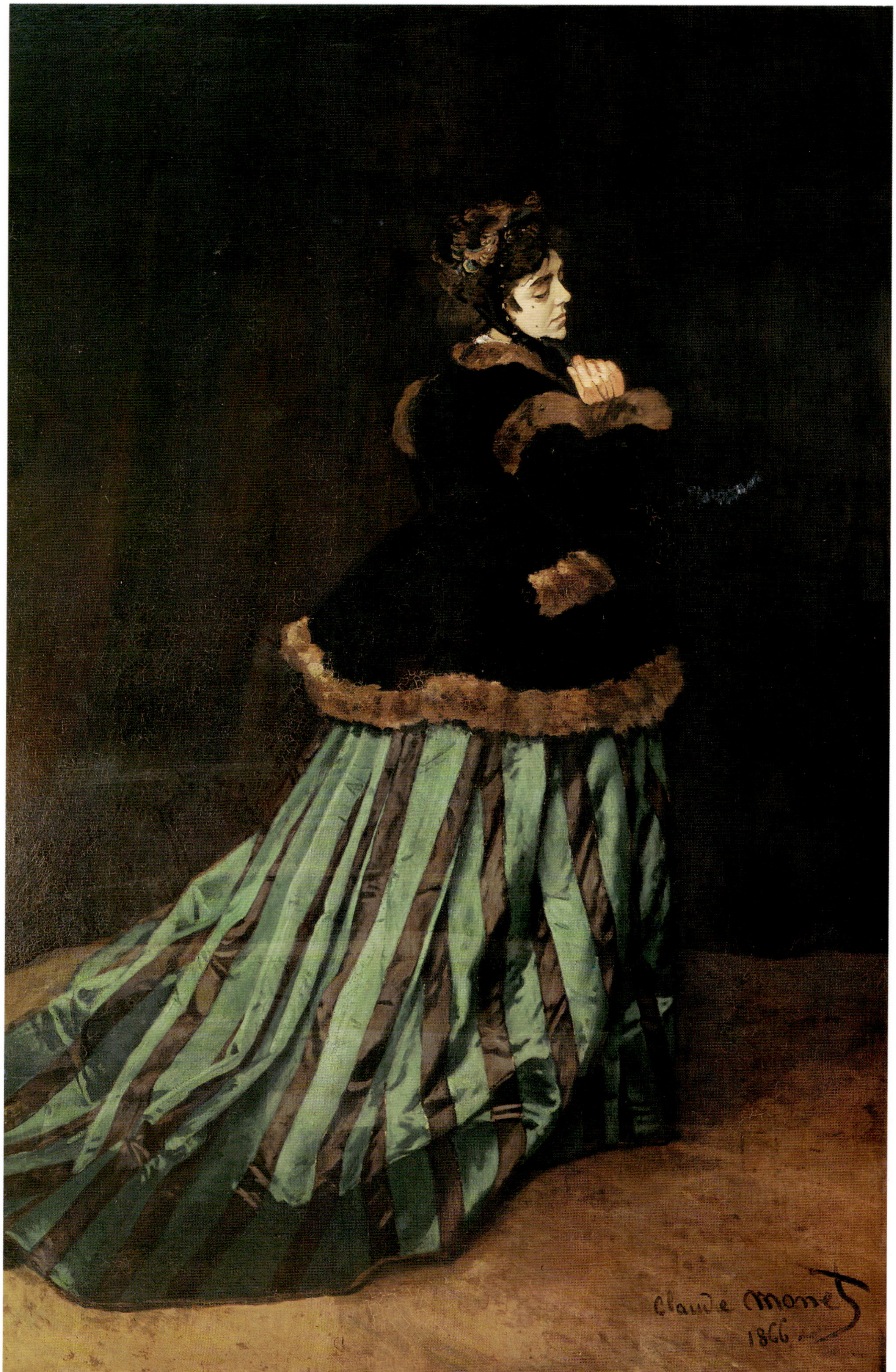
Claude Monet
1866

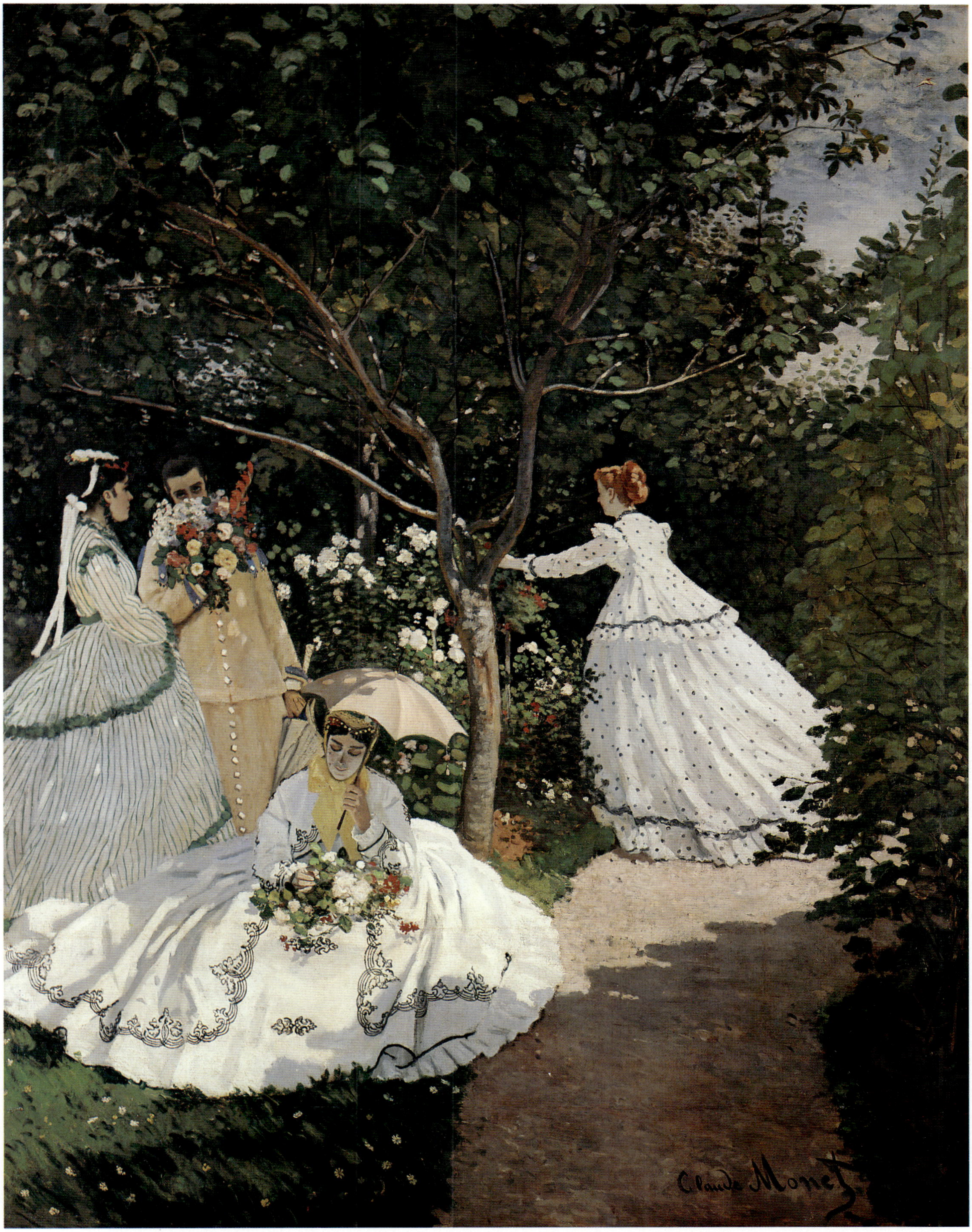

Opposite:
CAMILLE (THE GREEN DRESS), 1866
Oil on canvas, 91×59½in (231×151cm)
Kunsthalle, Bremen

Above:
WOMEN IN THE GARDEN, 1866-67
Oil on canvas, 100½×80¾in (255×205cm)
Musée d'Orsay, Paris

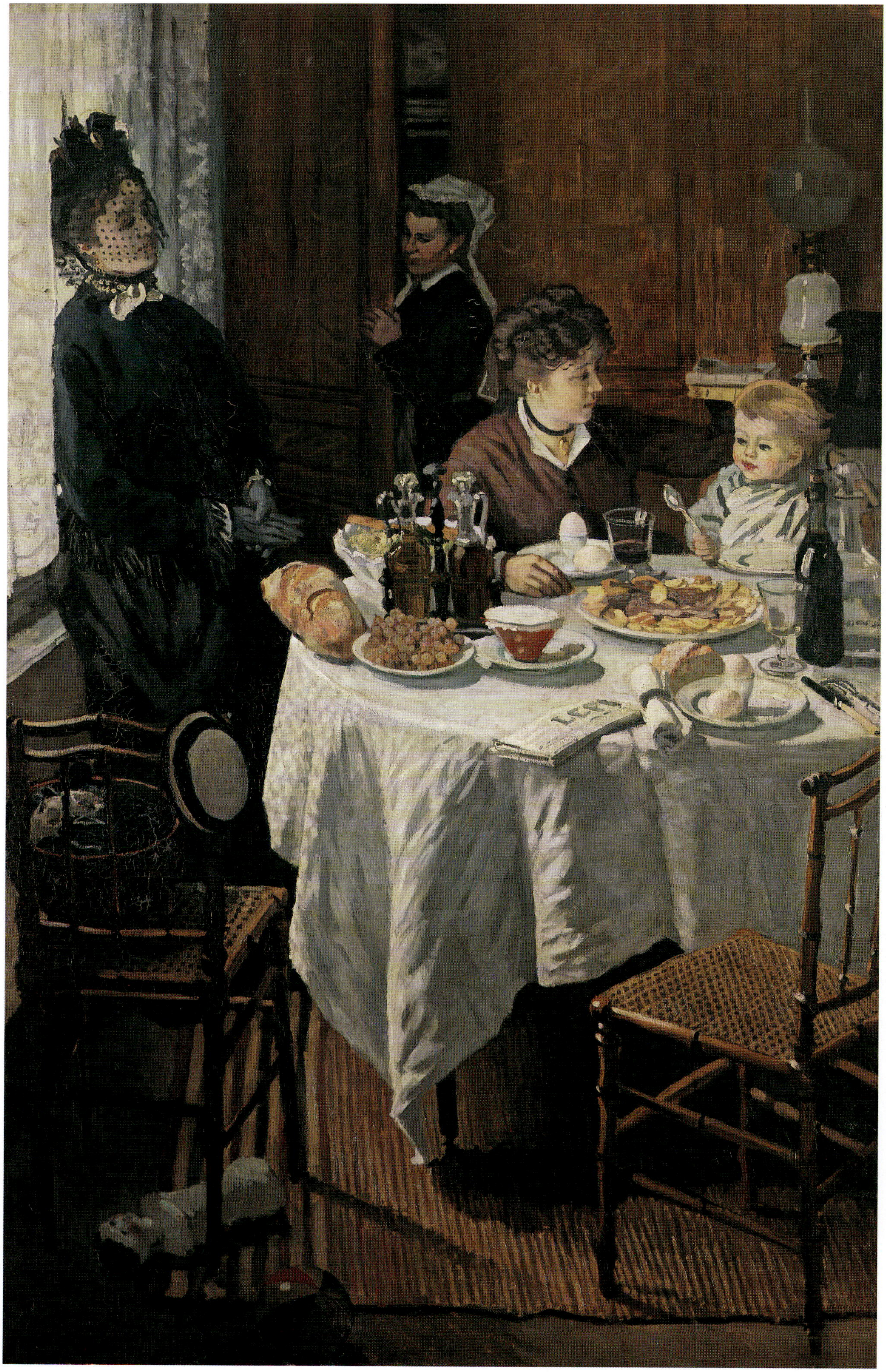

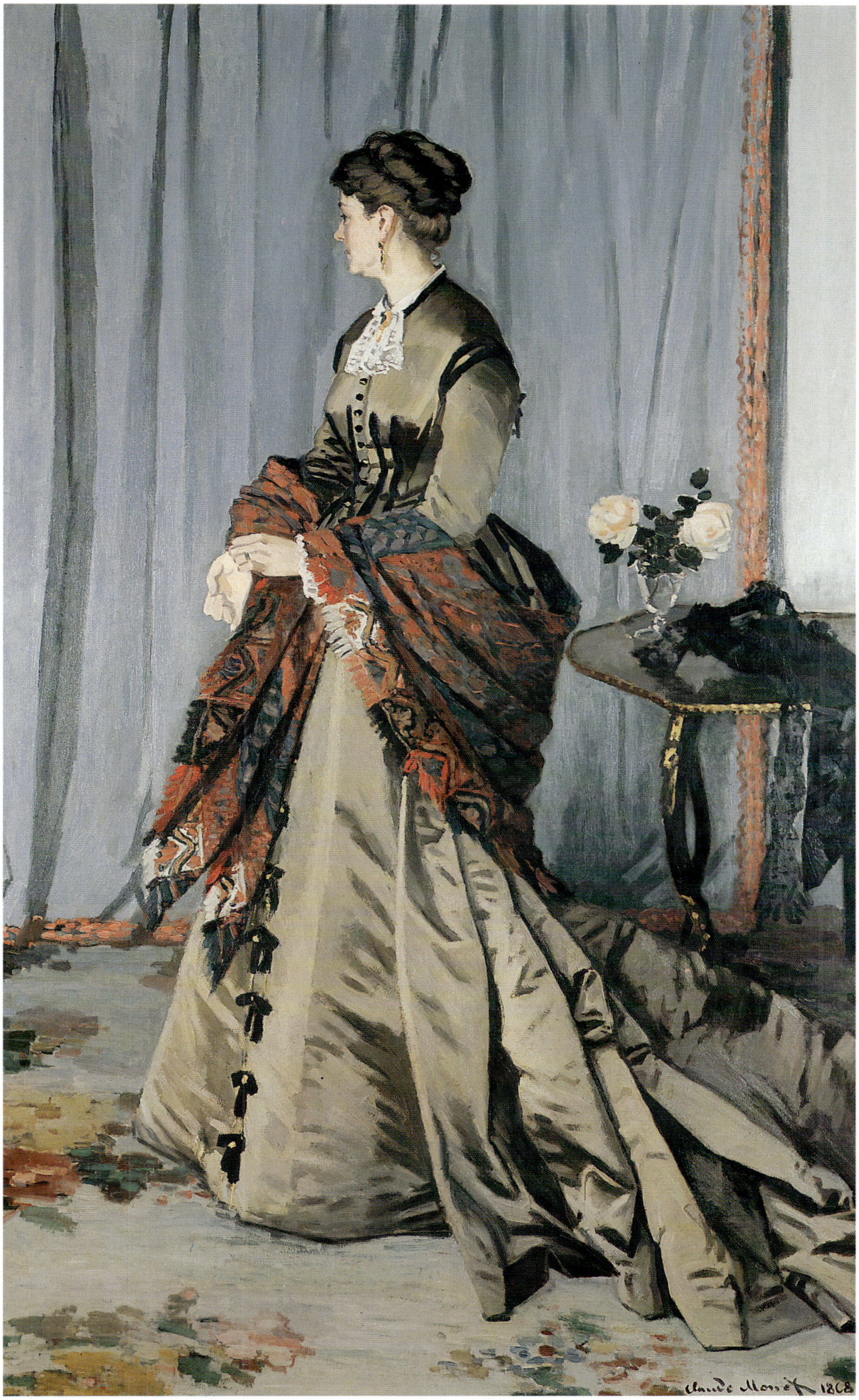

Opposite:
THE LUNCHEON, 1868
Oil on canvas, 90½×59½in (230×150cm)
Städelsches Kunstinstitut, Frankfurt

Above:
MADAME GAUDIBERT, 1868
Oil on canvas, 85×54½in (215.9×138.4cm)
Musée d'Orsay, Paris

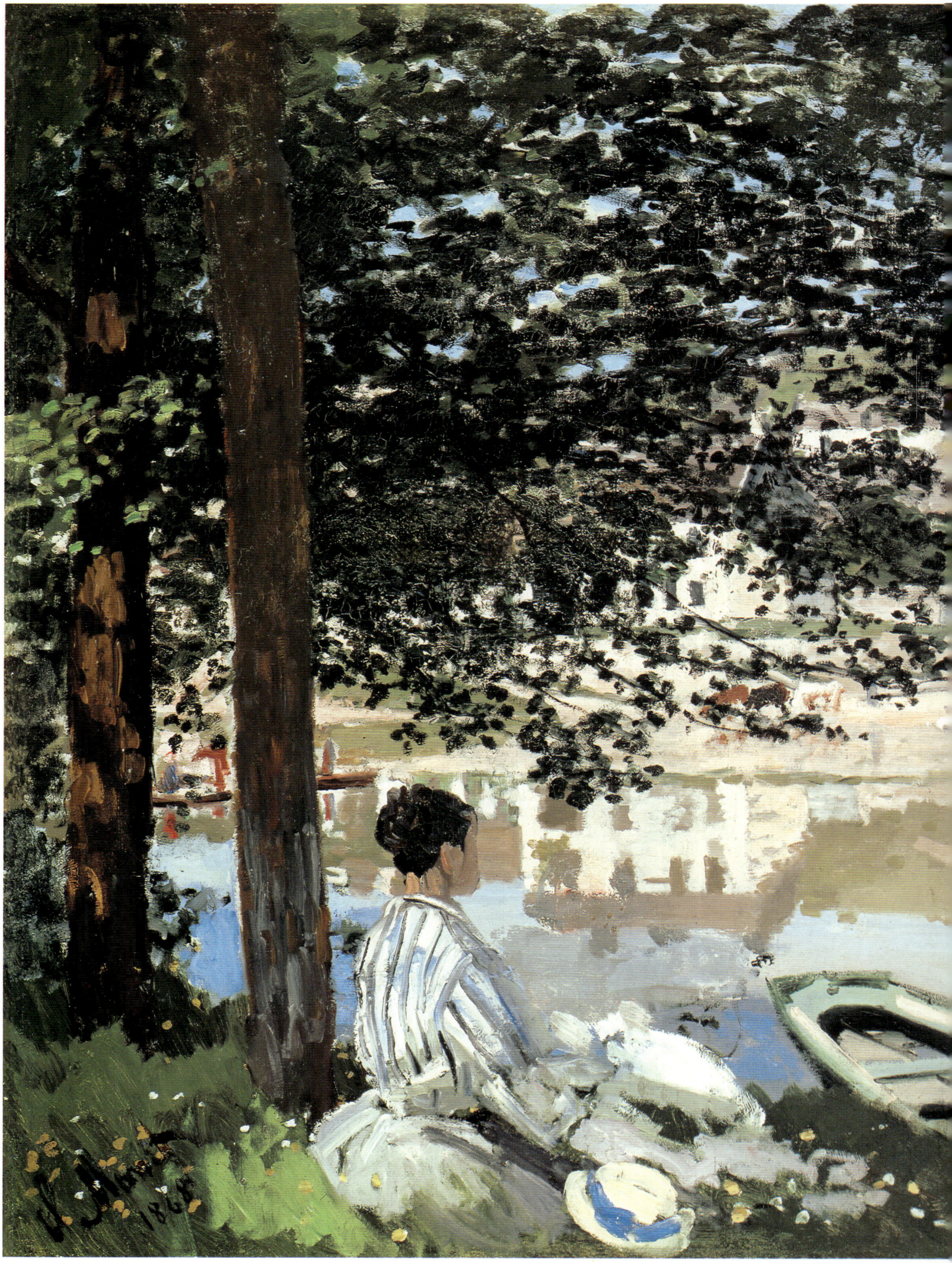

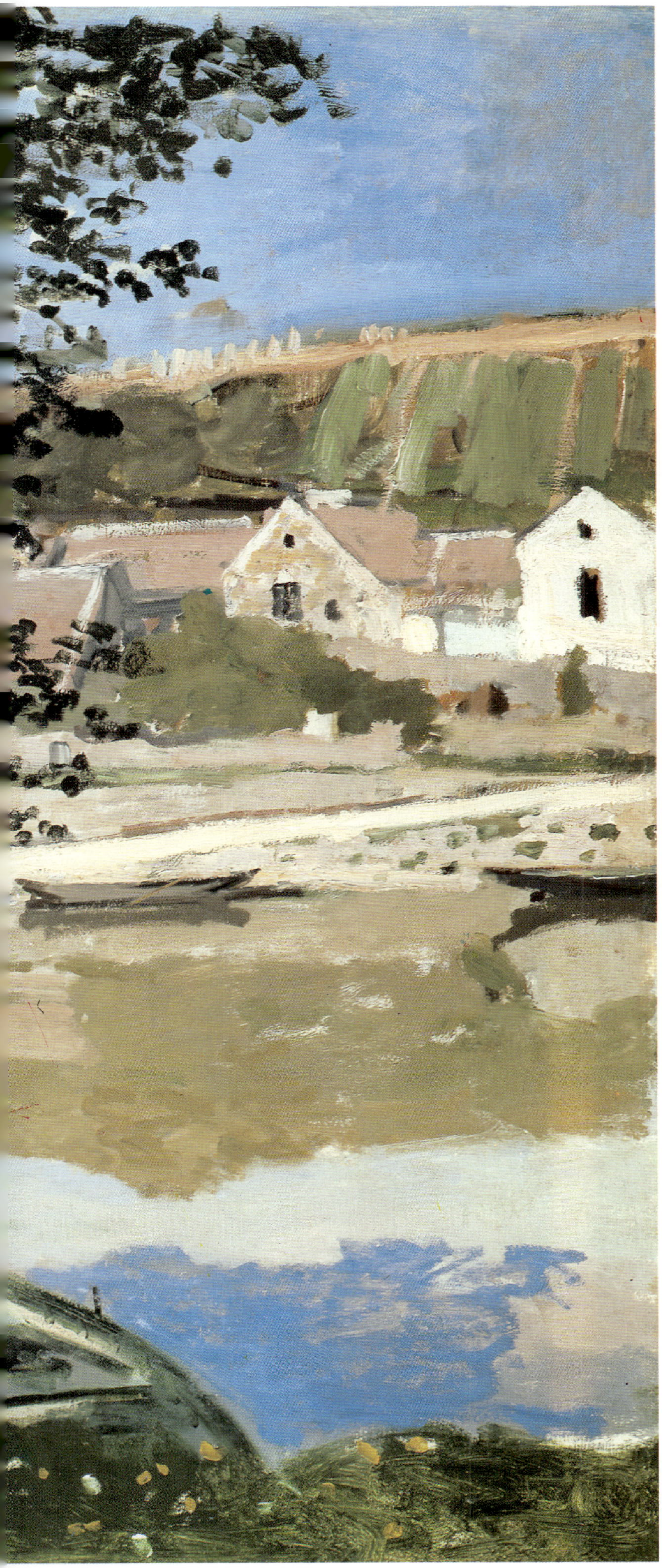

On the Seine at Bennecourt, 1868
Oil on canvas, 32×39¾in (81.5×100.7cm)
Art Institute of Chicago
Potter Palmer Collection

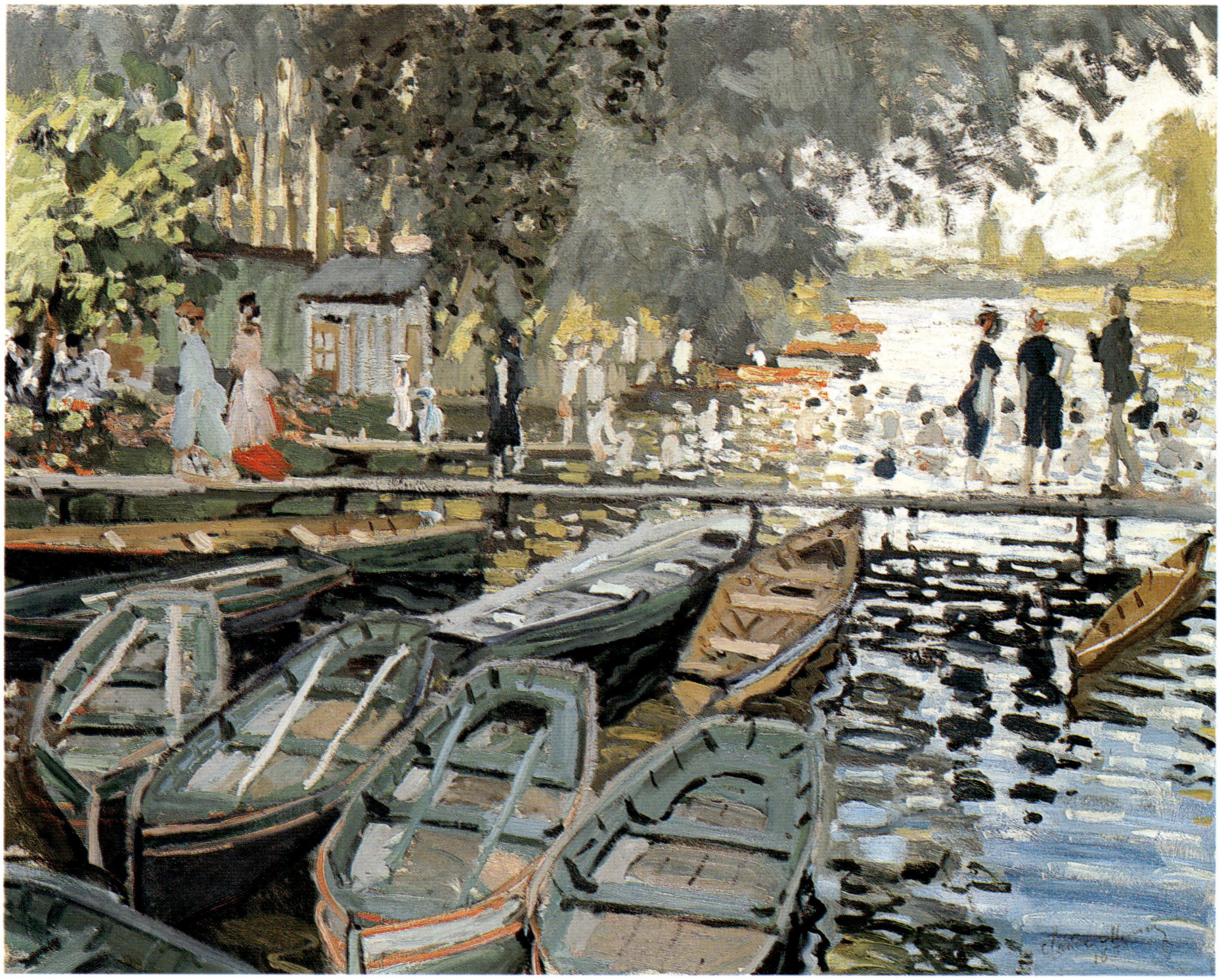

Above:
BATHERS AT LA GRENOUILLÈRE, 1869
Oil on canvas, 30¼×36¼in (77×92cm)
The National Gallery, London

Opposite:
THE HÔTEL DES ROCHES NOIRES AT TROUVILLE, 1870
Oil on canvas, 31½×21¾in (80×55cm)
Musée d'Orsay, Paris

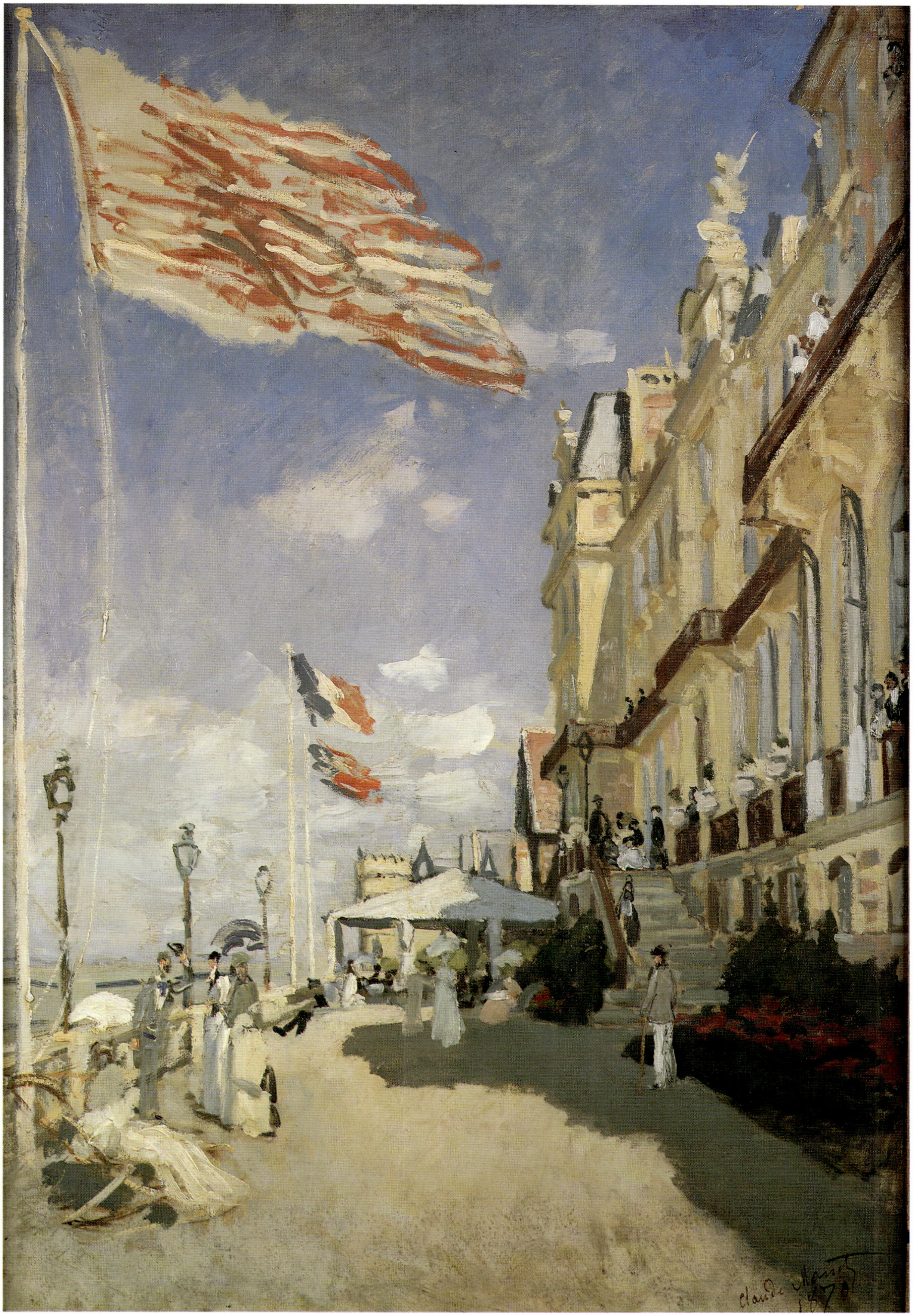

River Basin at Argenteuil, 1872
Oil on canvas, 23½×31¾in (60×80.5cm)
Musée d'Orsay, Paris

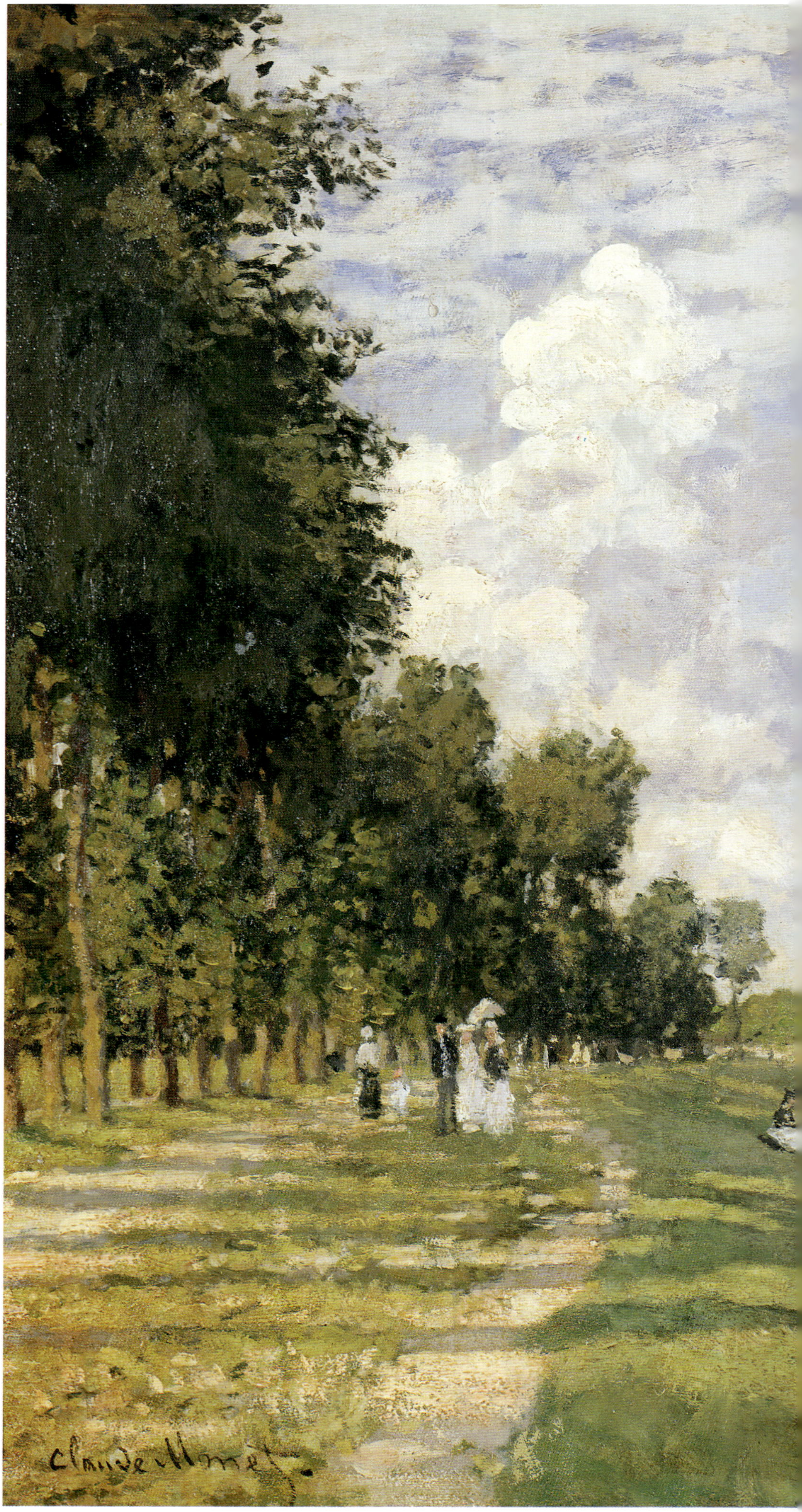

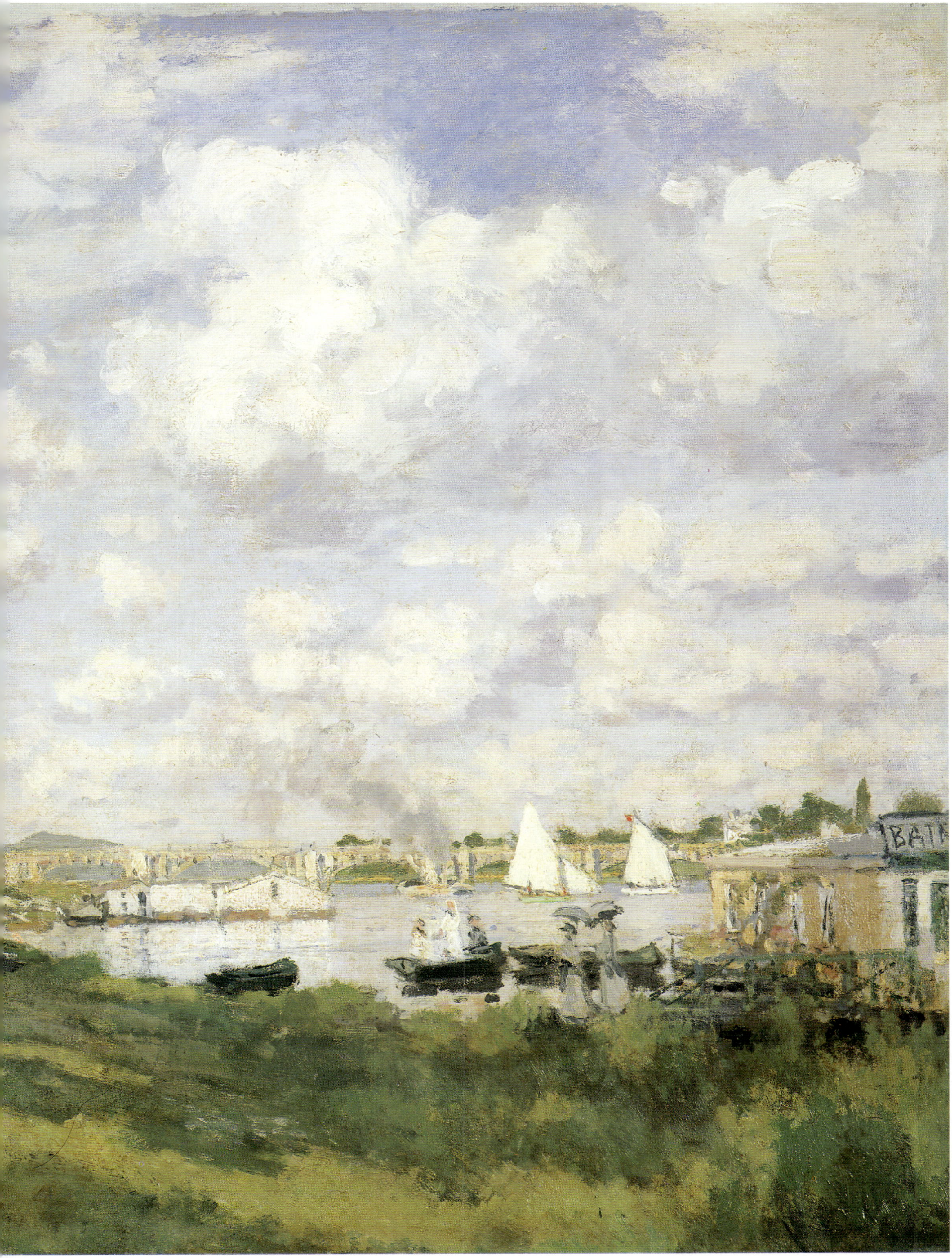

Impression: Sunrise, 1872
Oil on canvas, 19×24¾in (48×63cm)
Musée Marmottan, Paris

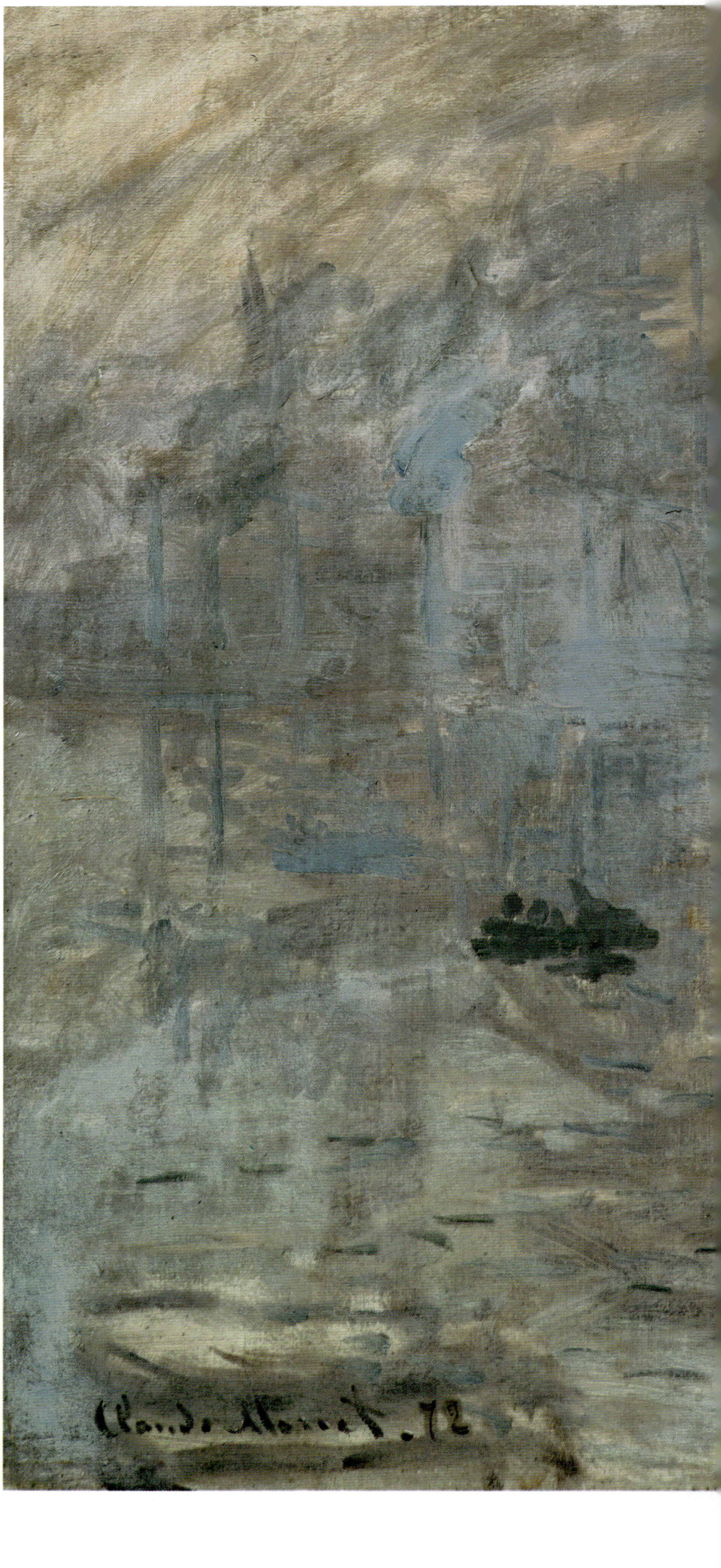

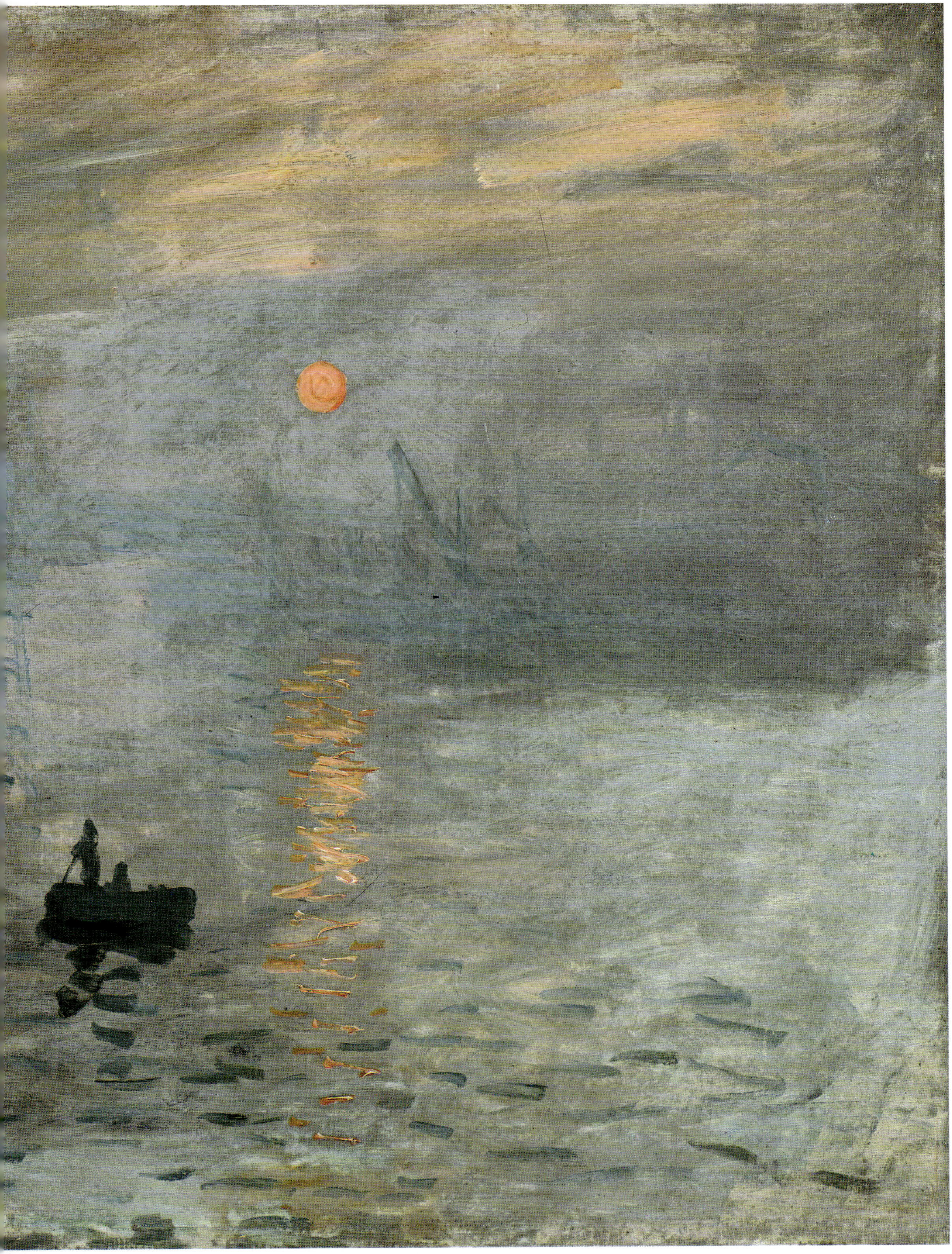

Wild Poppies, 1873
Oil on canvas, 19¾×25½in (50×65cm)
Musée d'Orsay, Paris

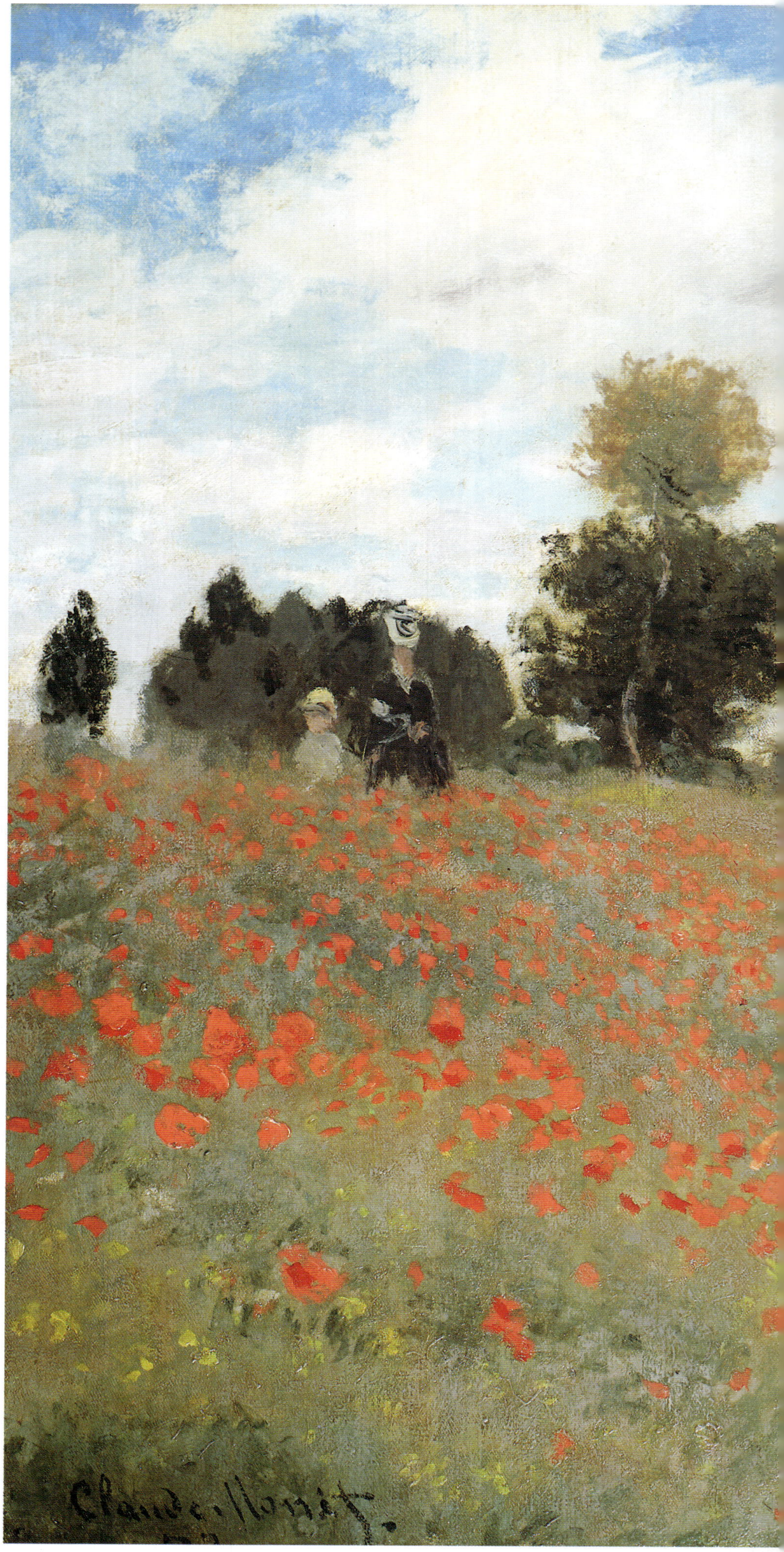

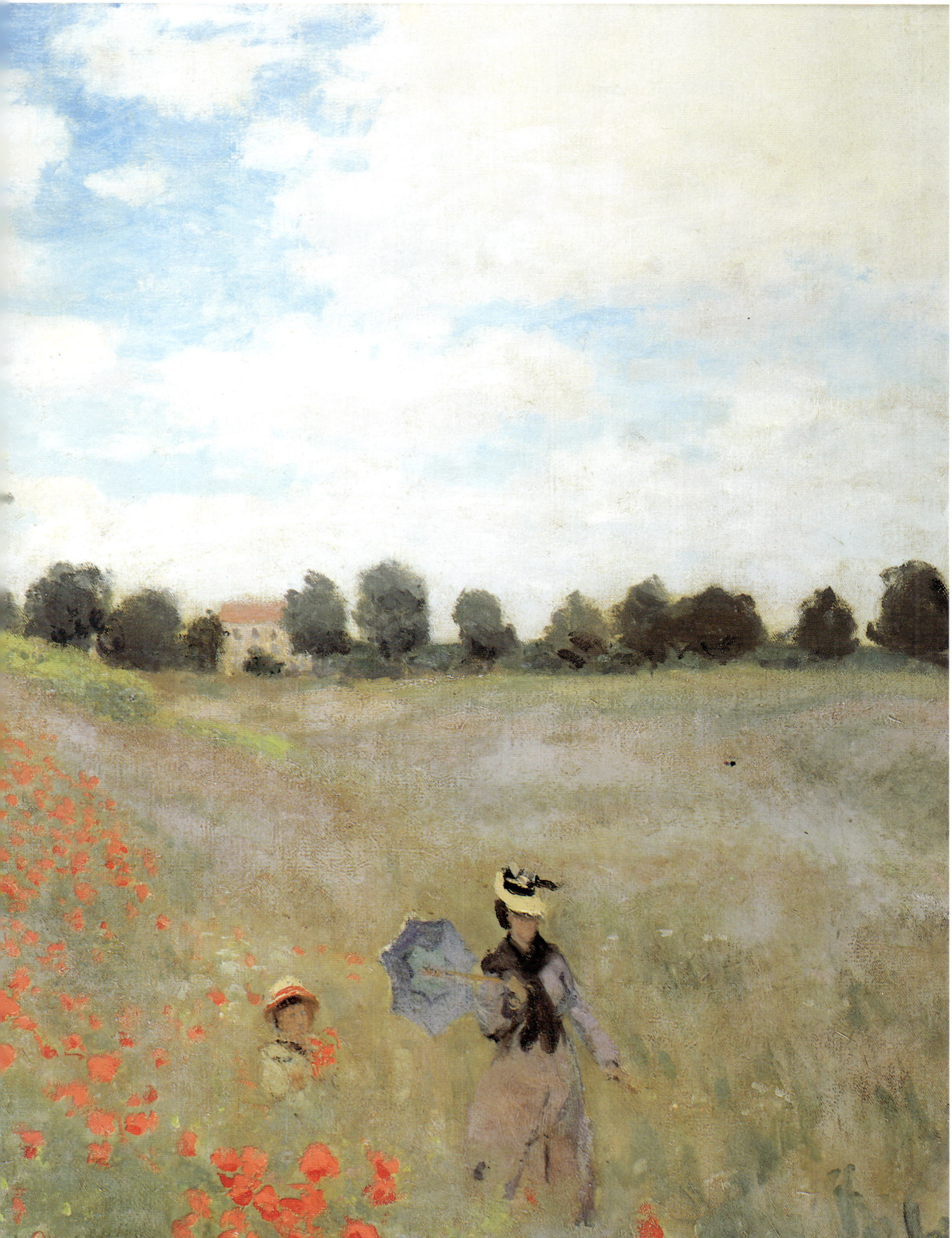

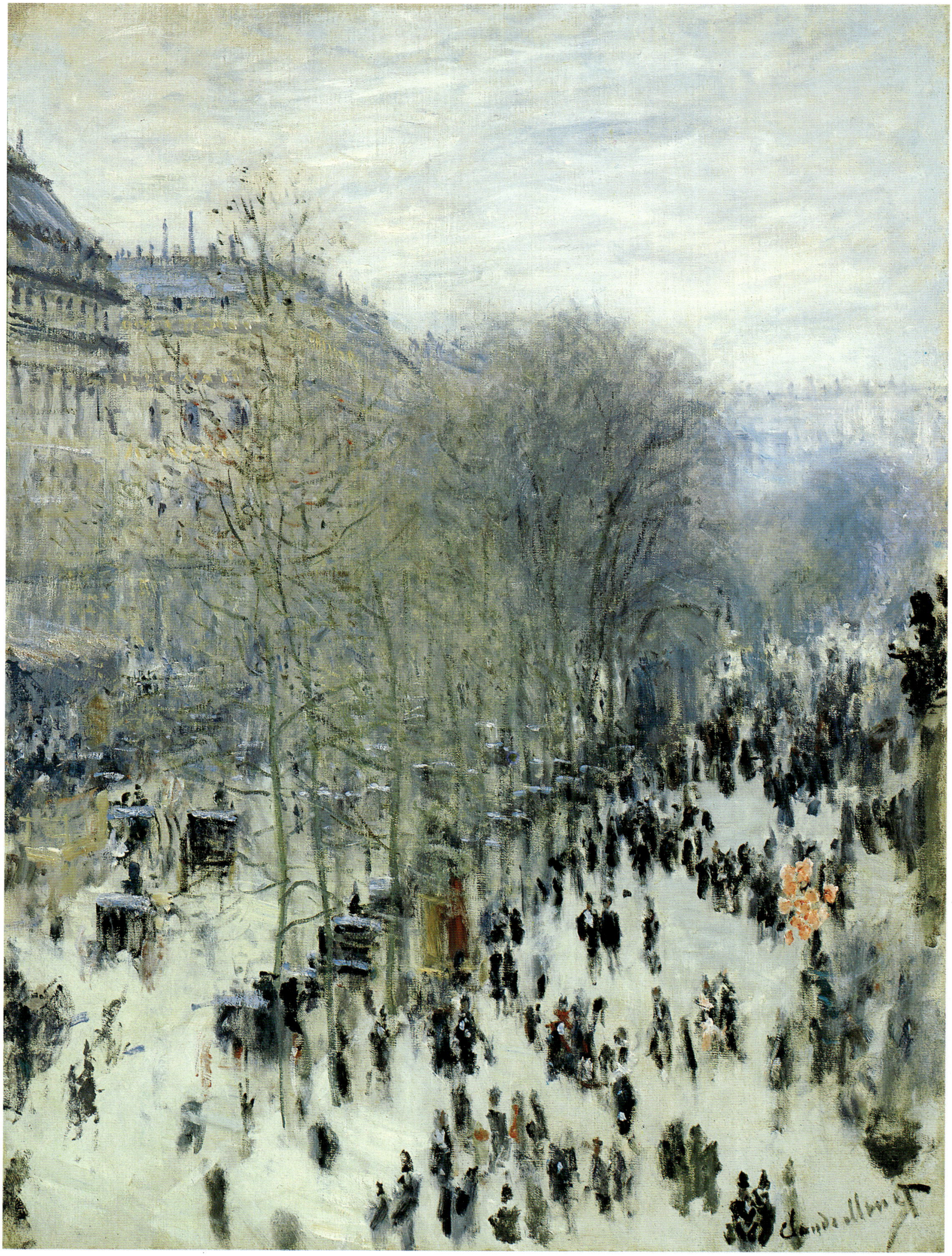

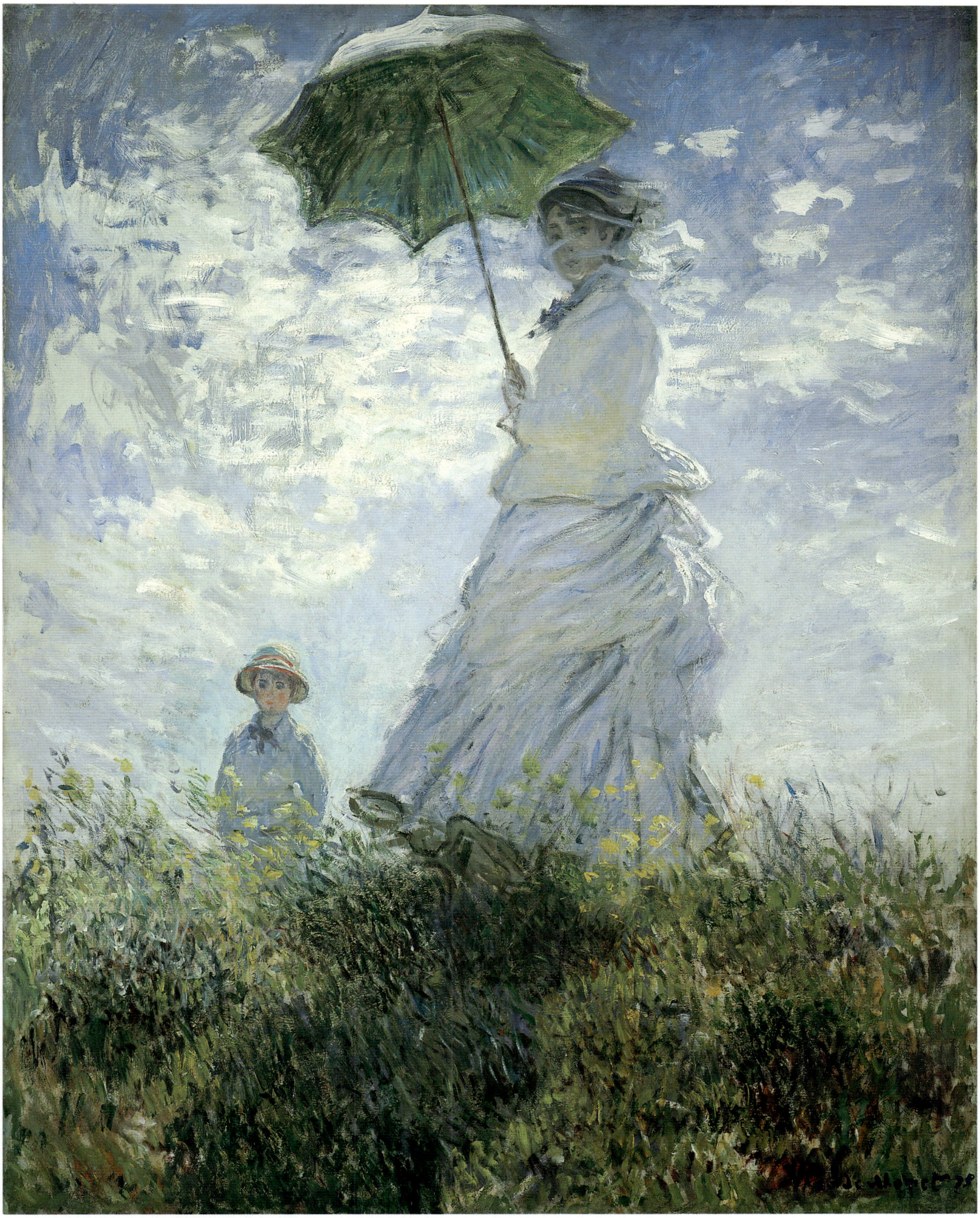

Opposite:
Boulevard des Capucines, 1873
Oil on canvas, 31½×23¼in (80×59cm)
The Nelson-Atkins Museum of Art, Kansas
Acquired through the Kenneth A and Helen F Spencer Foundation Acquisition Fund

Woman with a Parasol:
Madame Monet and Her Son, 1875
Oil on canvas, 39½×31¼in (100×81cm)
National Gallery of Art, Washington
Collection of Mr and Mrs Paul Melton

THE GARE SAINT-LAZARE, 1877
Oil on canvas, 29¾×41in (75.5×104cm)
Musée d'Orsay, Paris

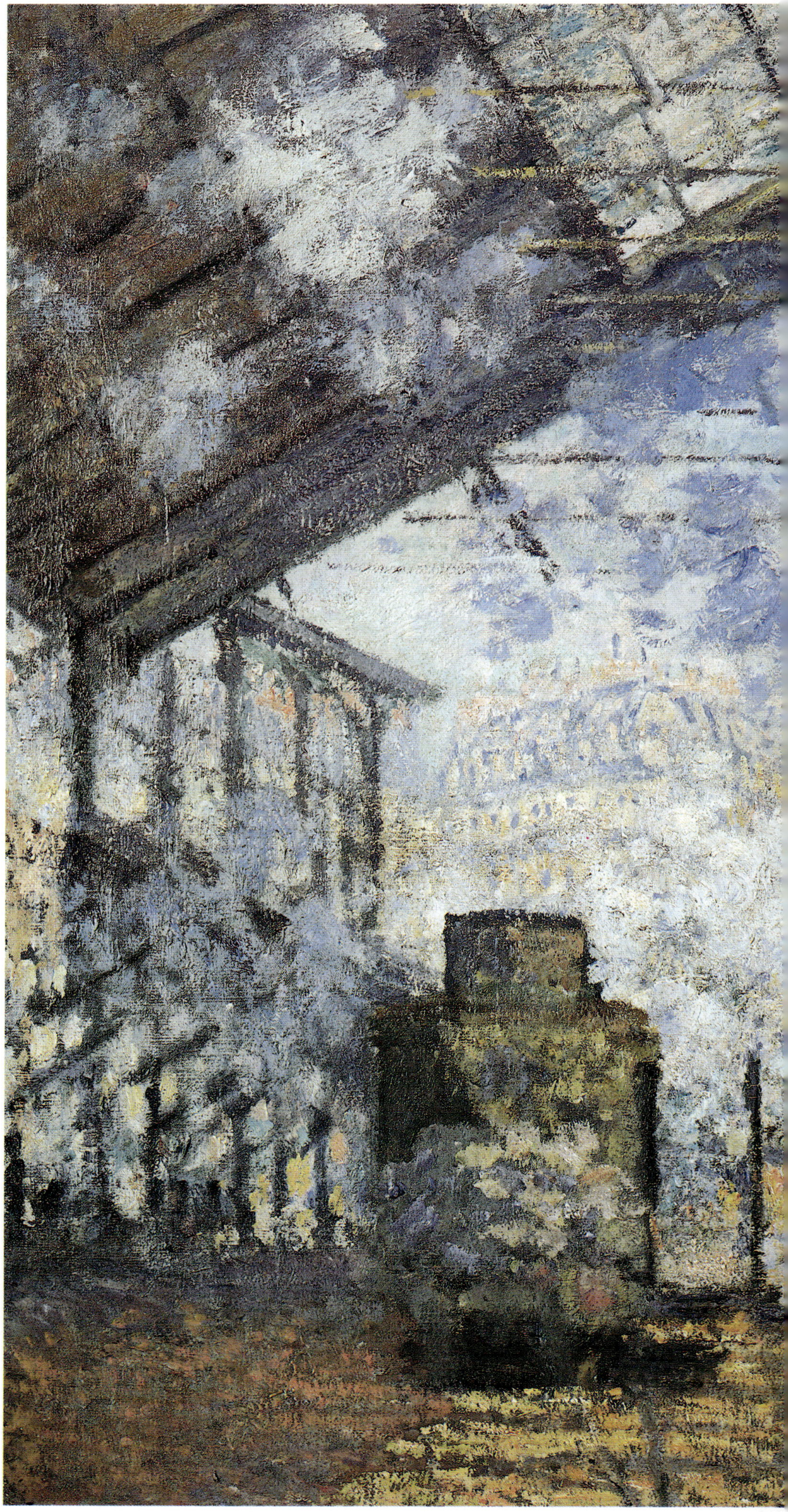

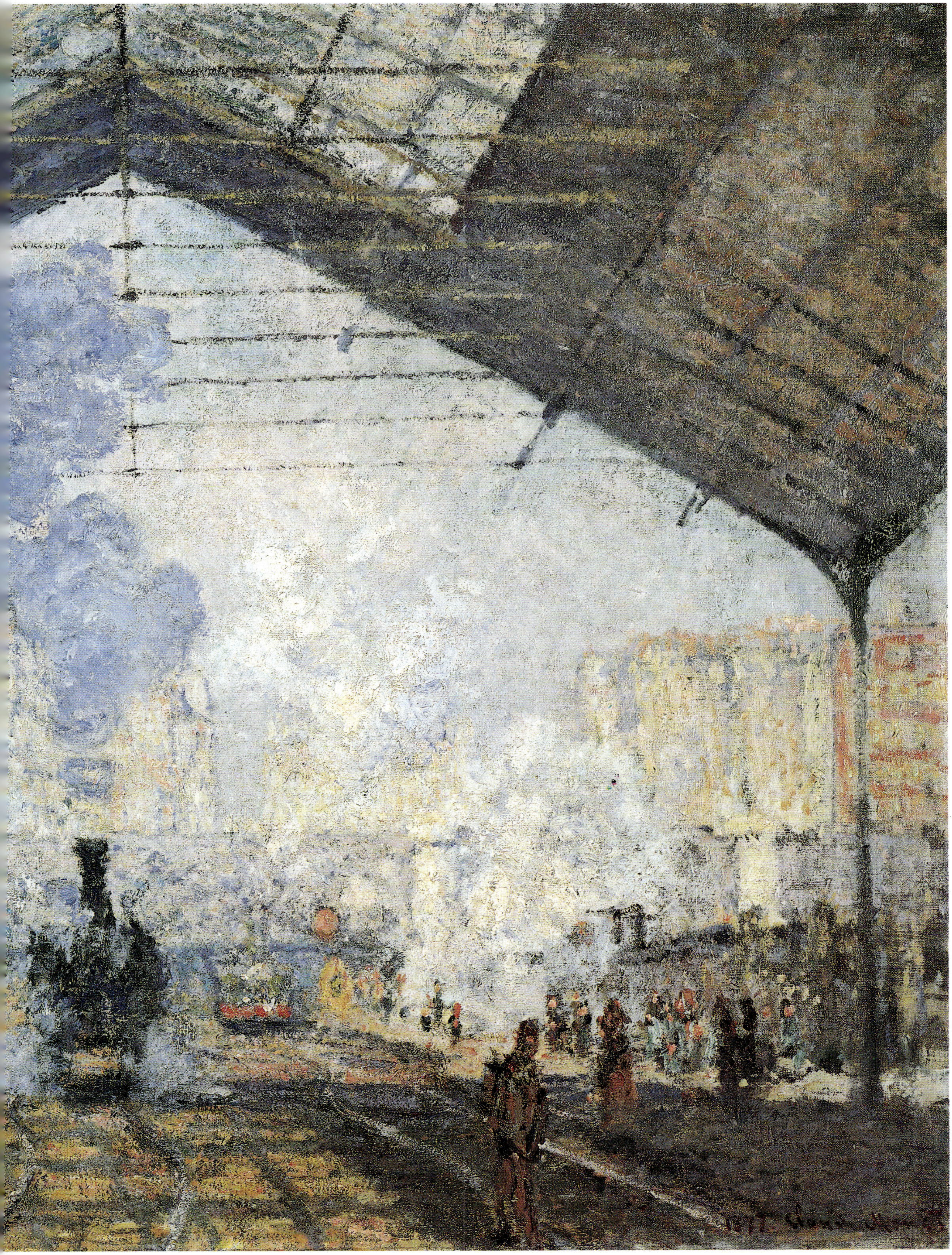

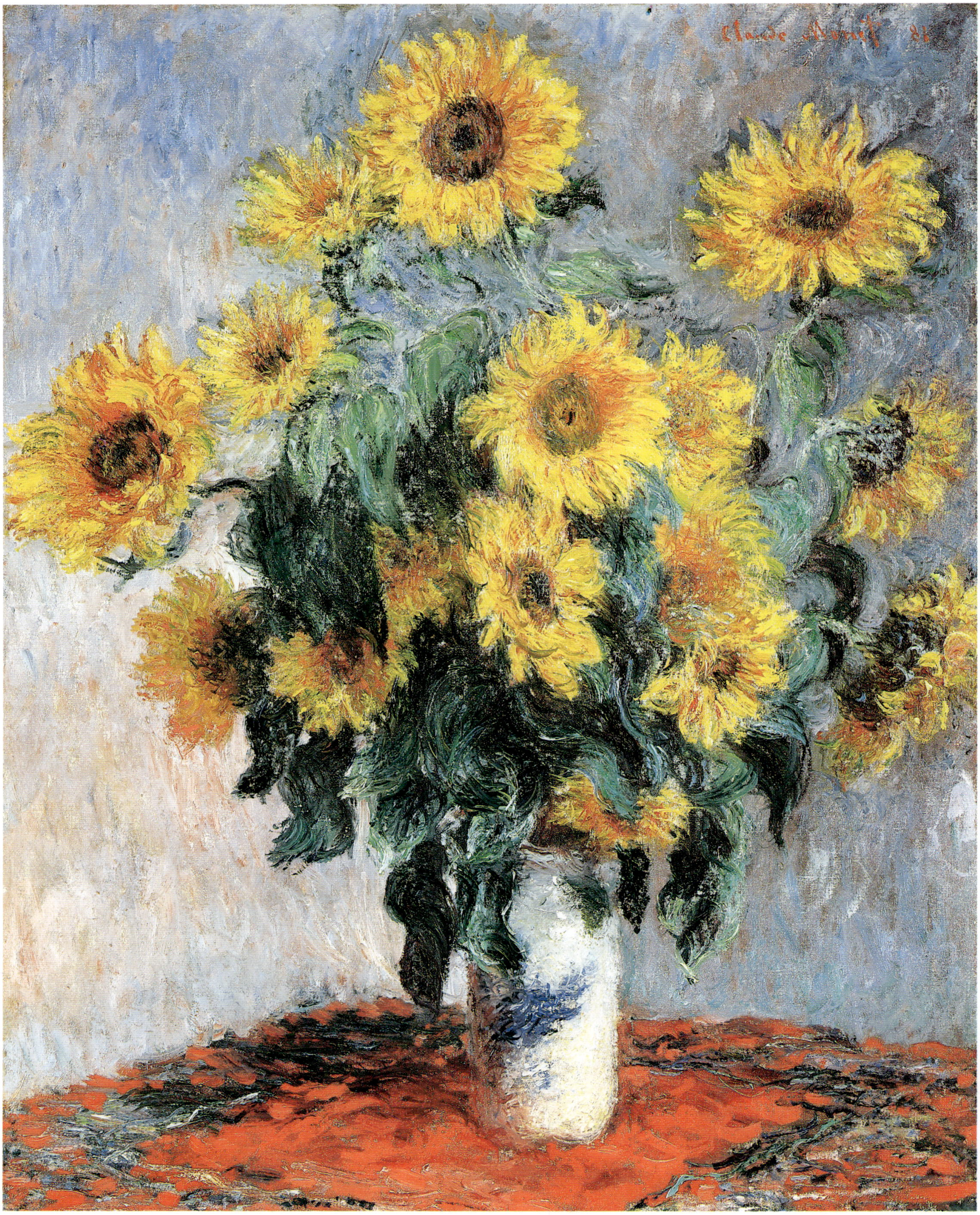

BOUQUET OF SUNFLOWERS, 1880-81
Oil on canvas, 39¾×32in (101×81.3cm)
Metropolitan Museum of Art, New York

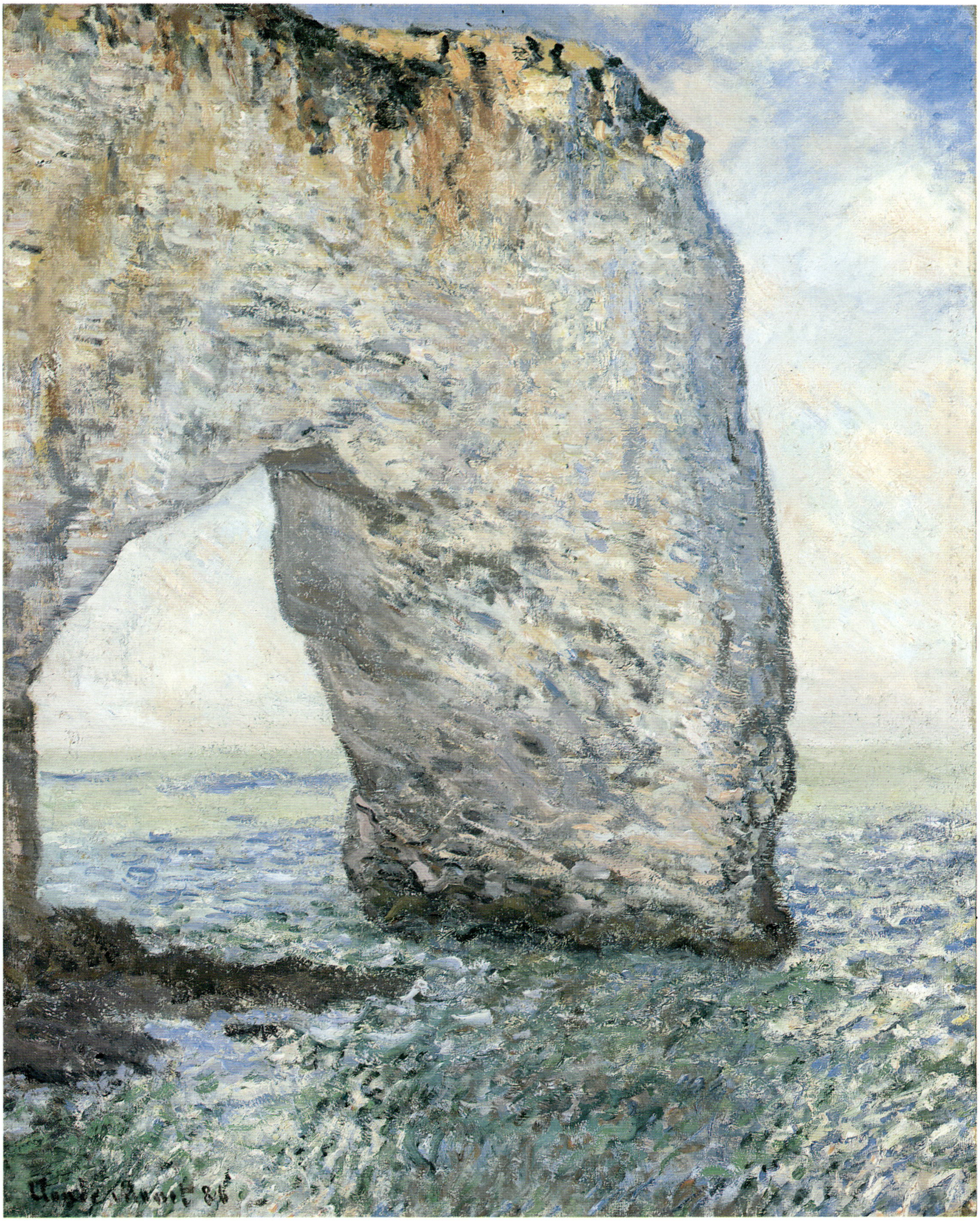

The Manneporte, 1886
Oil on canvas, 32×25¾in (81.3×65.4cm)
Metropolitan Museum of Art, New York
Bequest of Lillie P Bliss, 1931

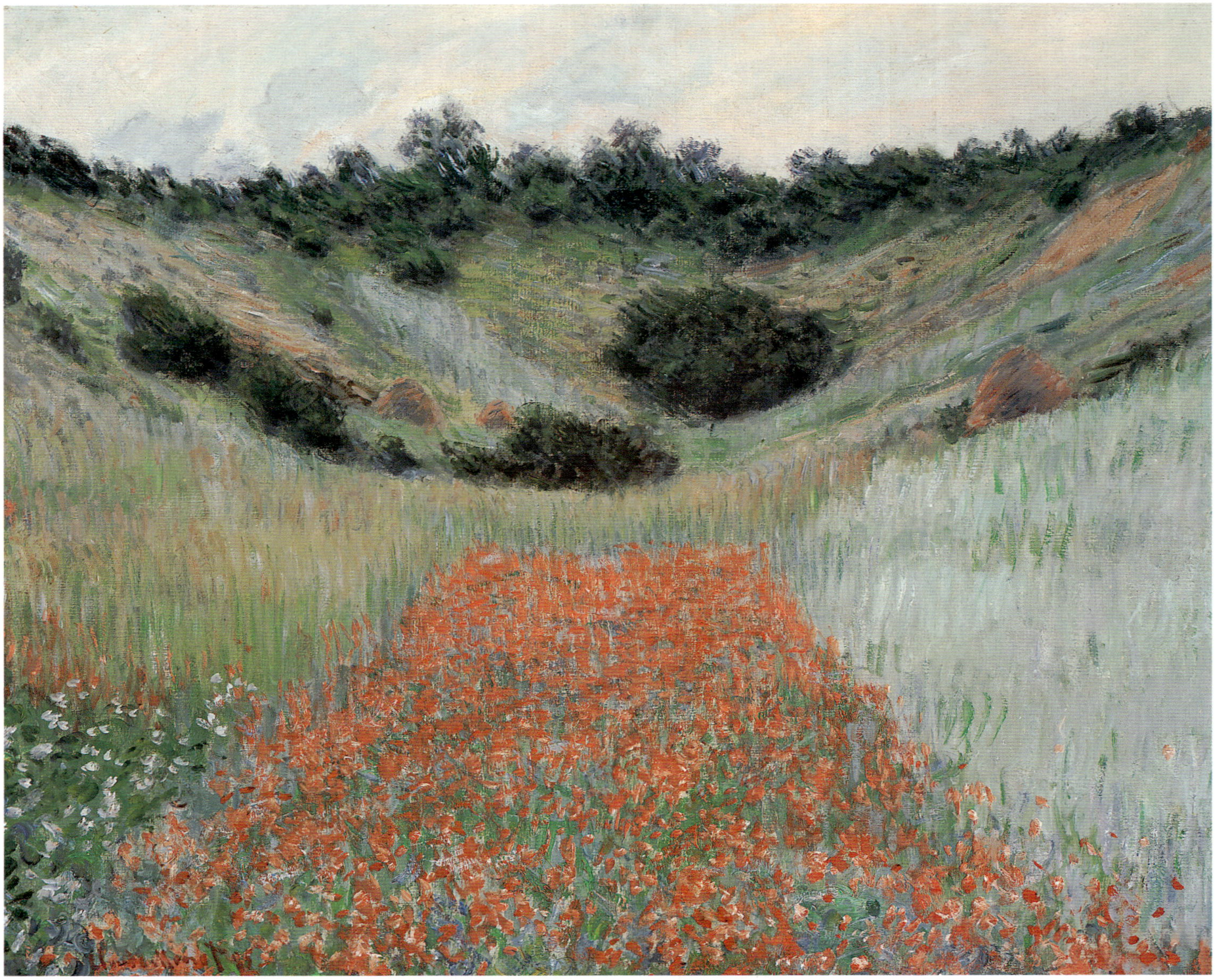

Poppy Field near Giverny, 1885
Oil on canvas, 25½×32in (65×81cm)
Museum of Fine Arts, Boston
Bequest of Robert J Edwards and Gift of Hannah Mary Edwards and Grace M Edwards in memory of their mother

GRAINSTACKS AT SUNSET, 1891
Oil on canvas, 25¾×36½in (73.3×92.6cm)
Museum of Fine Arts, Boston
Julia Cheney Edwards Collection

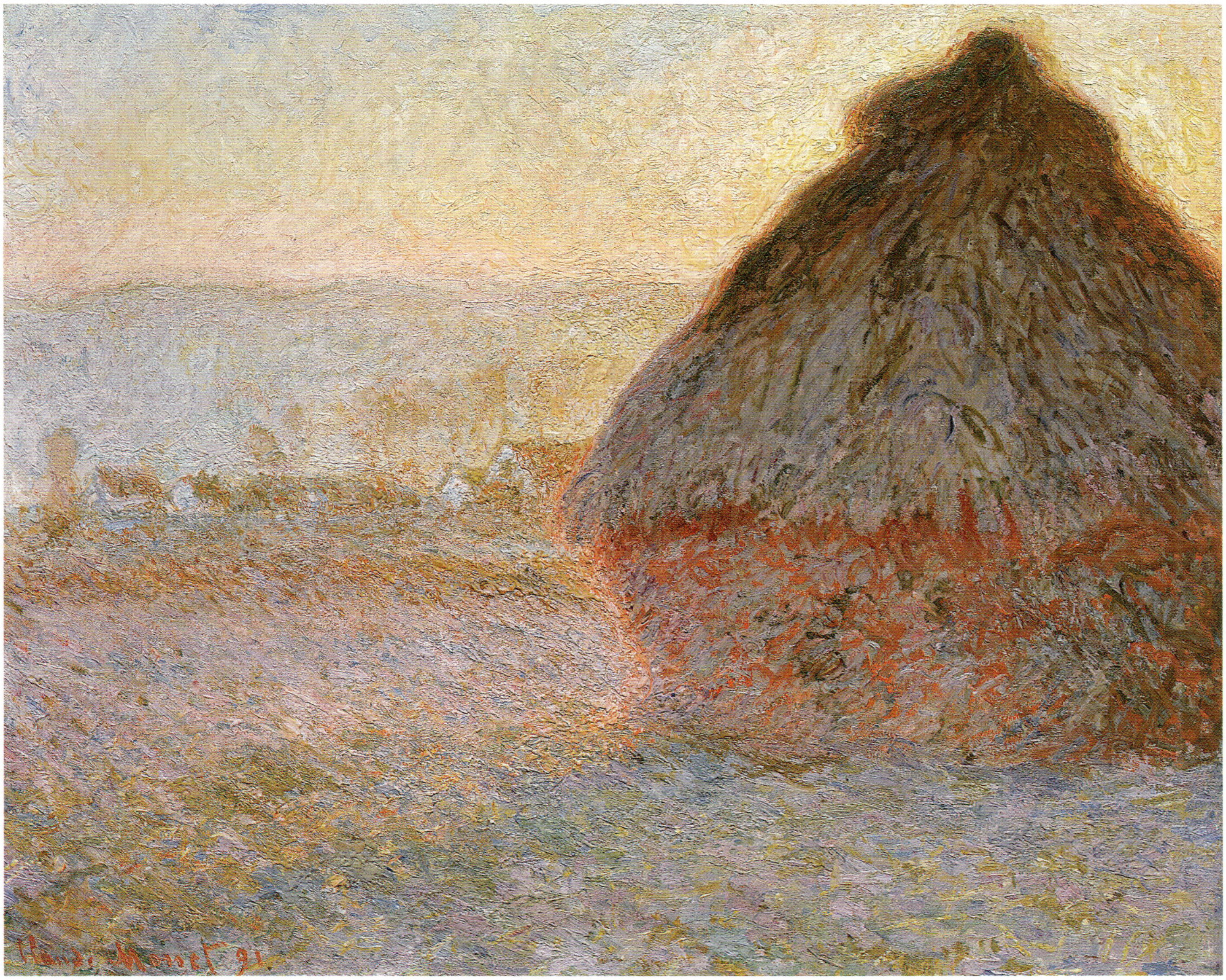

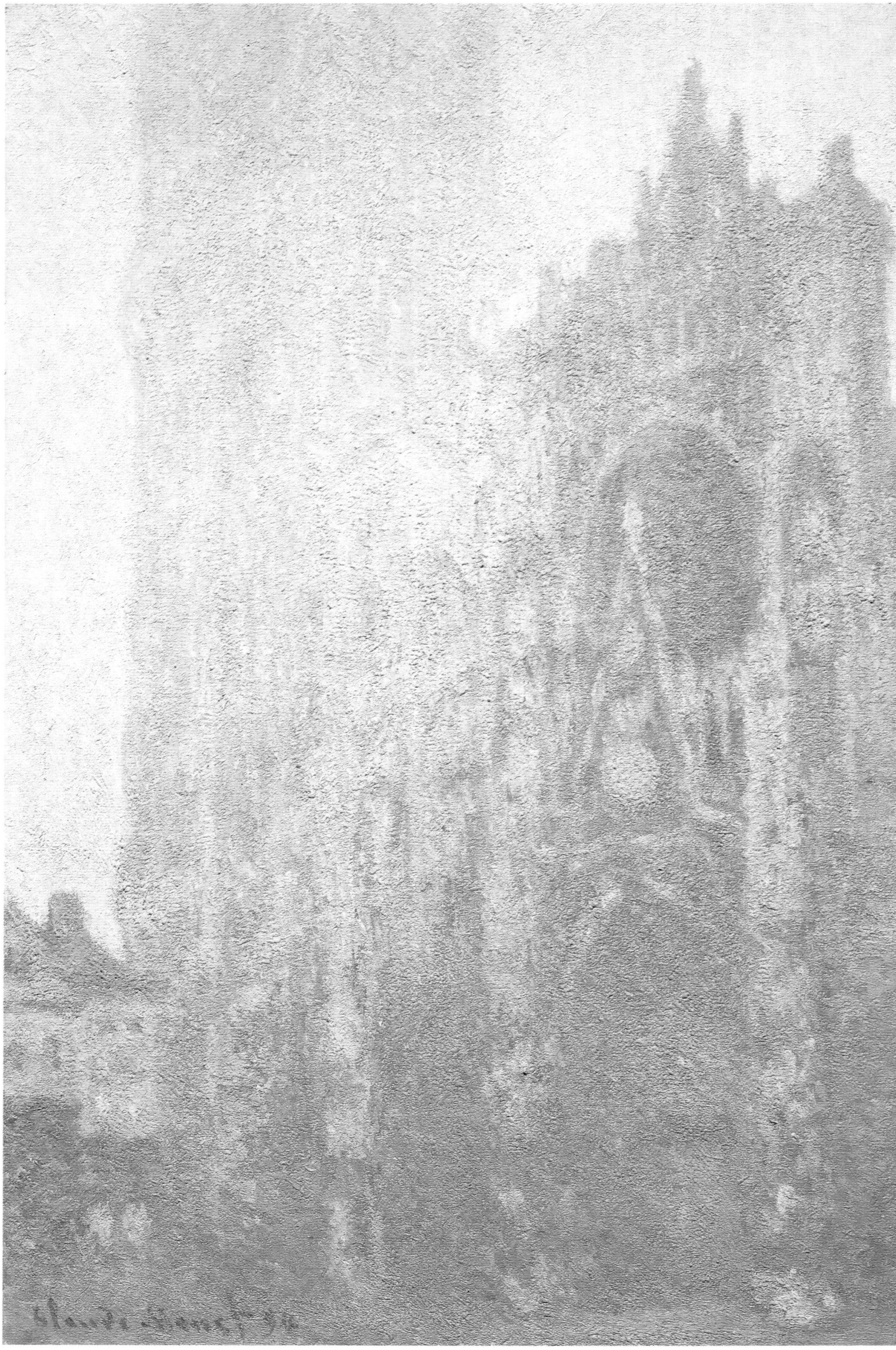

ROUEN CATHEDRAL: TOUR D'ALBANE, EARLY MORNING, 1894
Oil on canvas, 41¾×29in (105×73.7cm)
Museum of Fine Arts, Boston

ROUEN CATHEDRAL AT SUNSET, 1894
Oil on canvas, 39¼×25½in (100×65cm)
Musée Marmottan, Paris

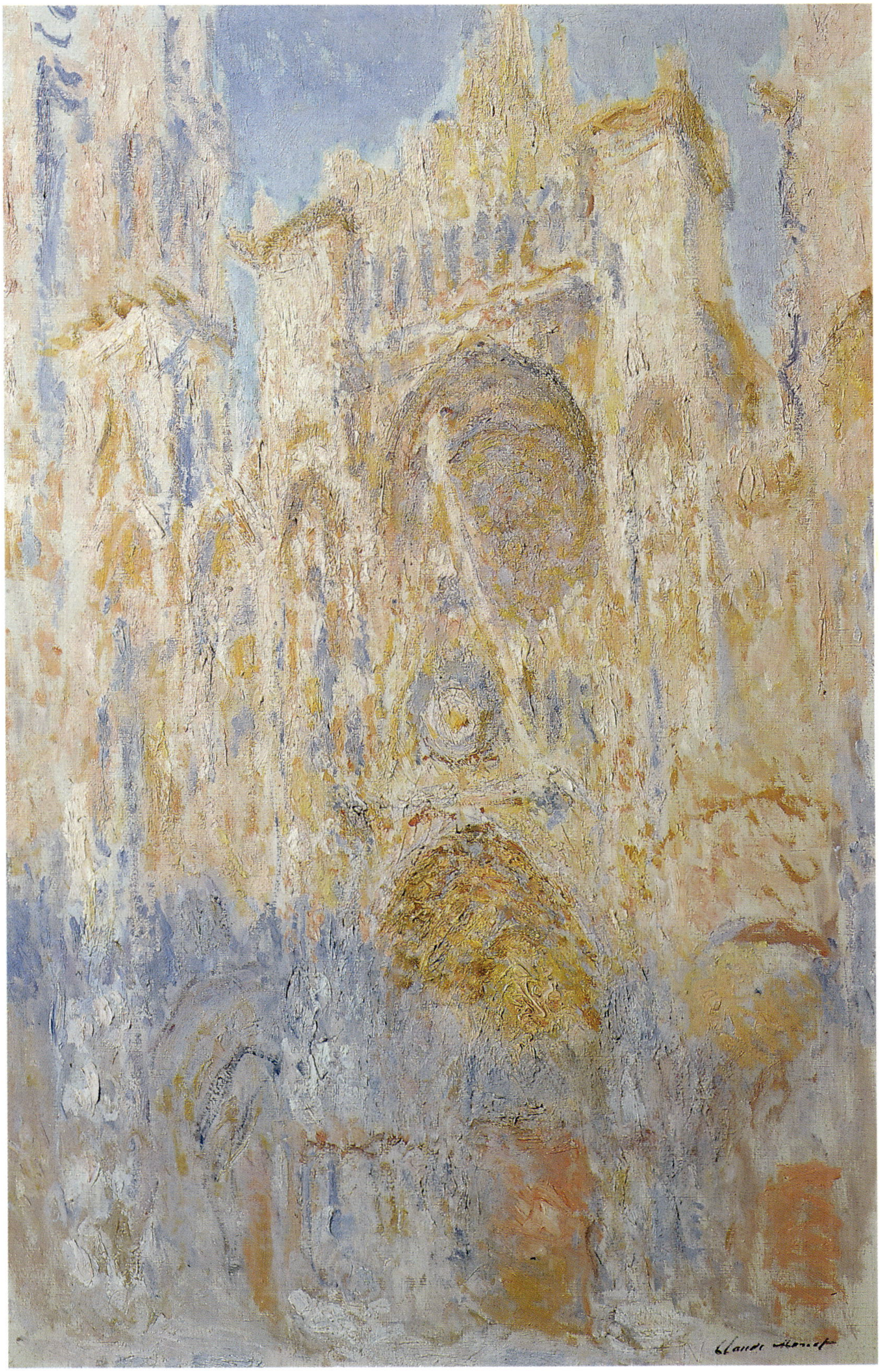

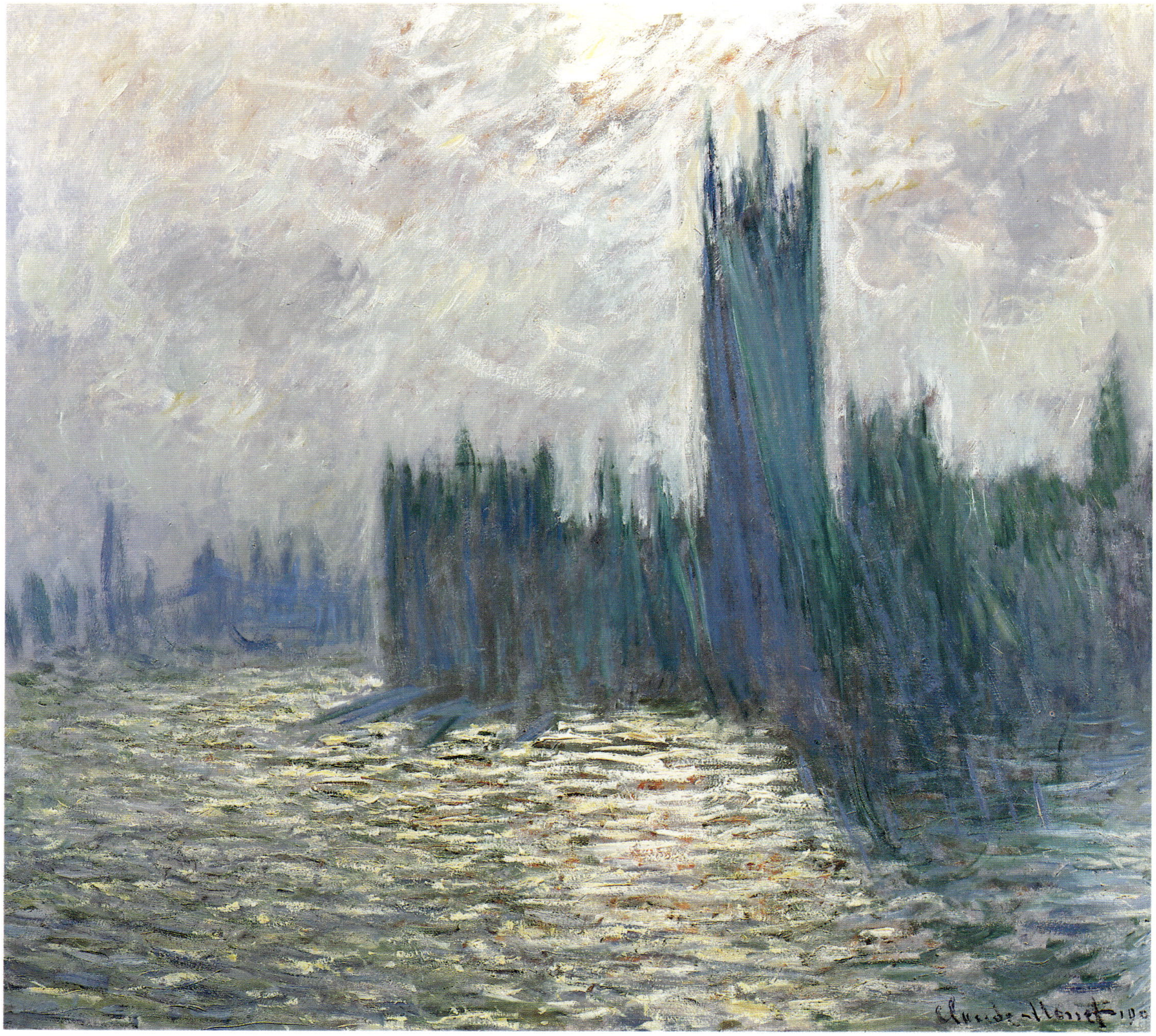

LONDON, HOUSES OF PARLIAMENT, 1905
Oil on canvas, 31¾×36¼in (81×92cm)
Musée Marmottan, Paris

THE DARIO PALACE, VENICE, 1908
Oil on canvas, 36¼×28¾in (92×73cm)
National Museum of Wales, Cardiff

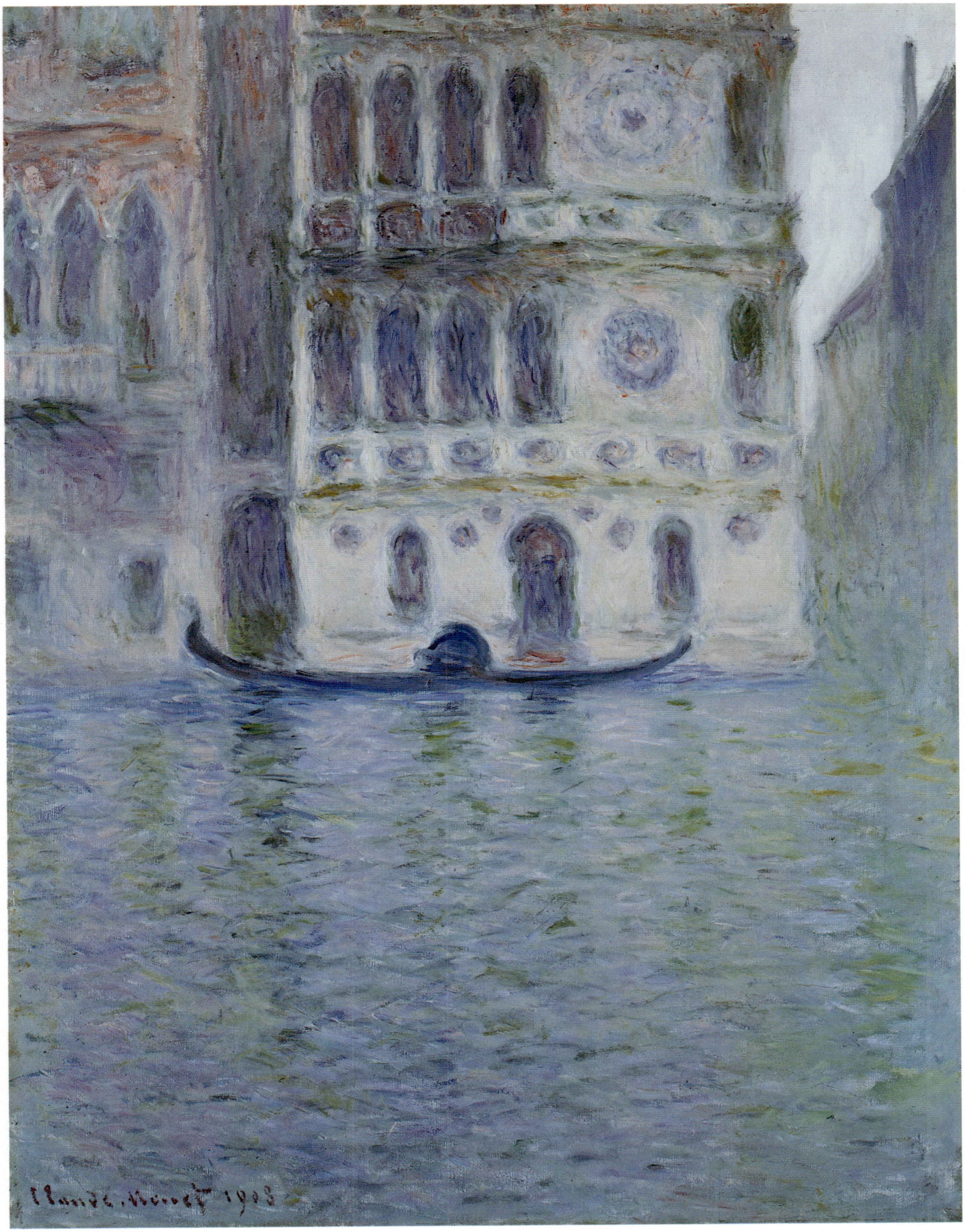

THE JAPANESE BRIDGE (LE BASSIN AUX NYMPHÉAS), 1899
Oil on canvas, 34¾×36¼in (88.2×92cm)
The National Gallery, London

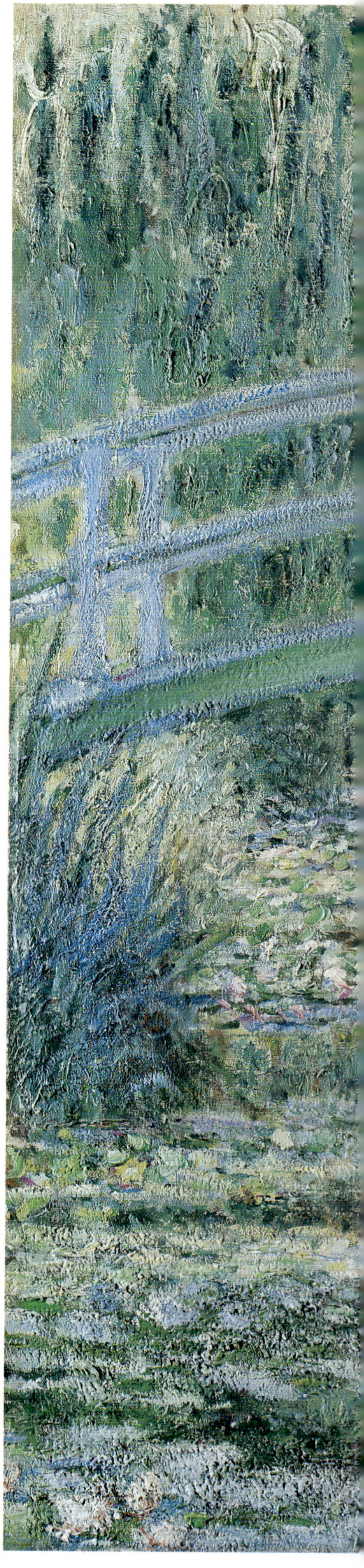

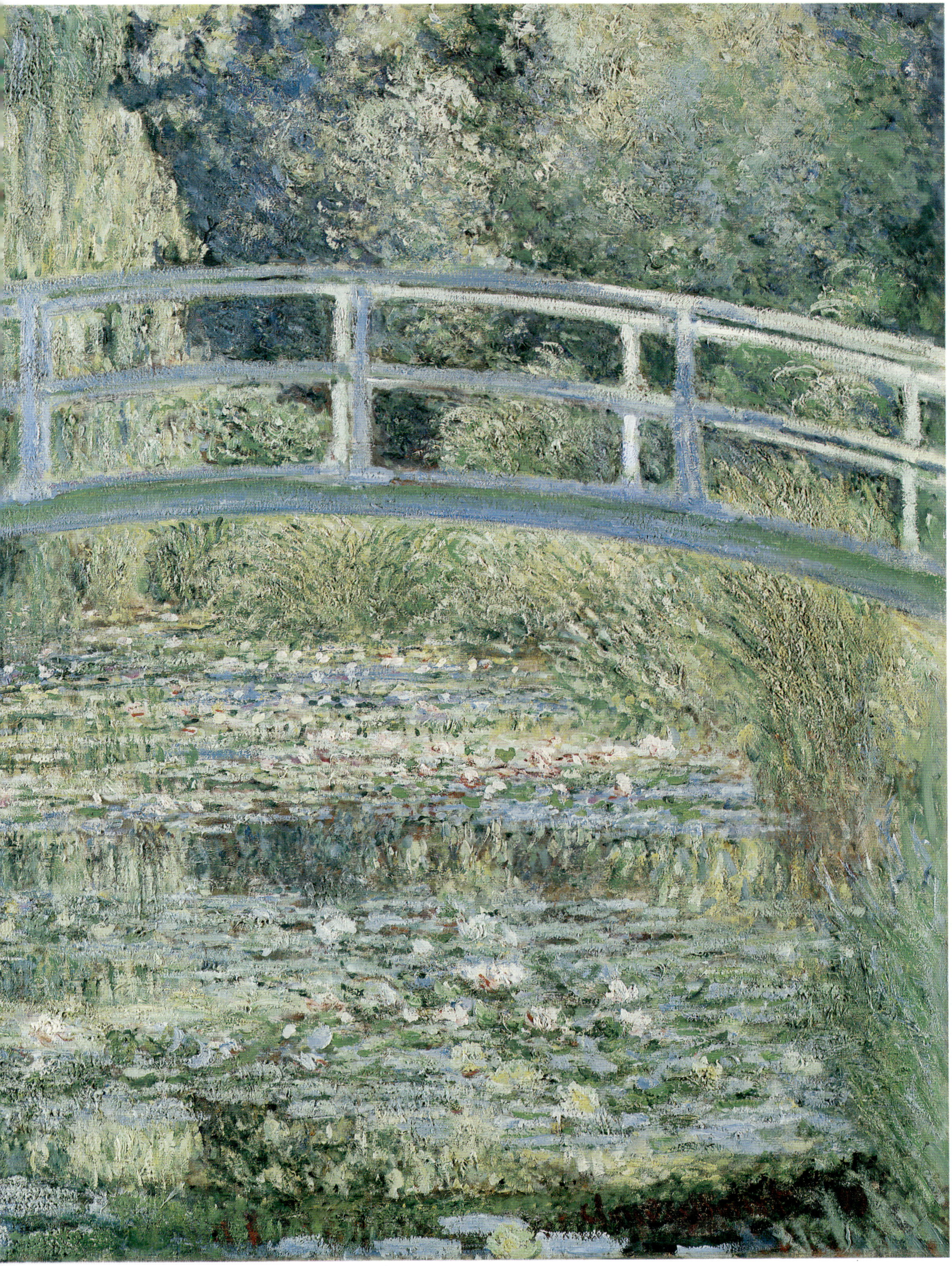

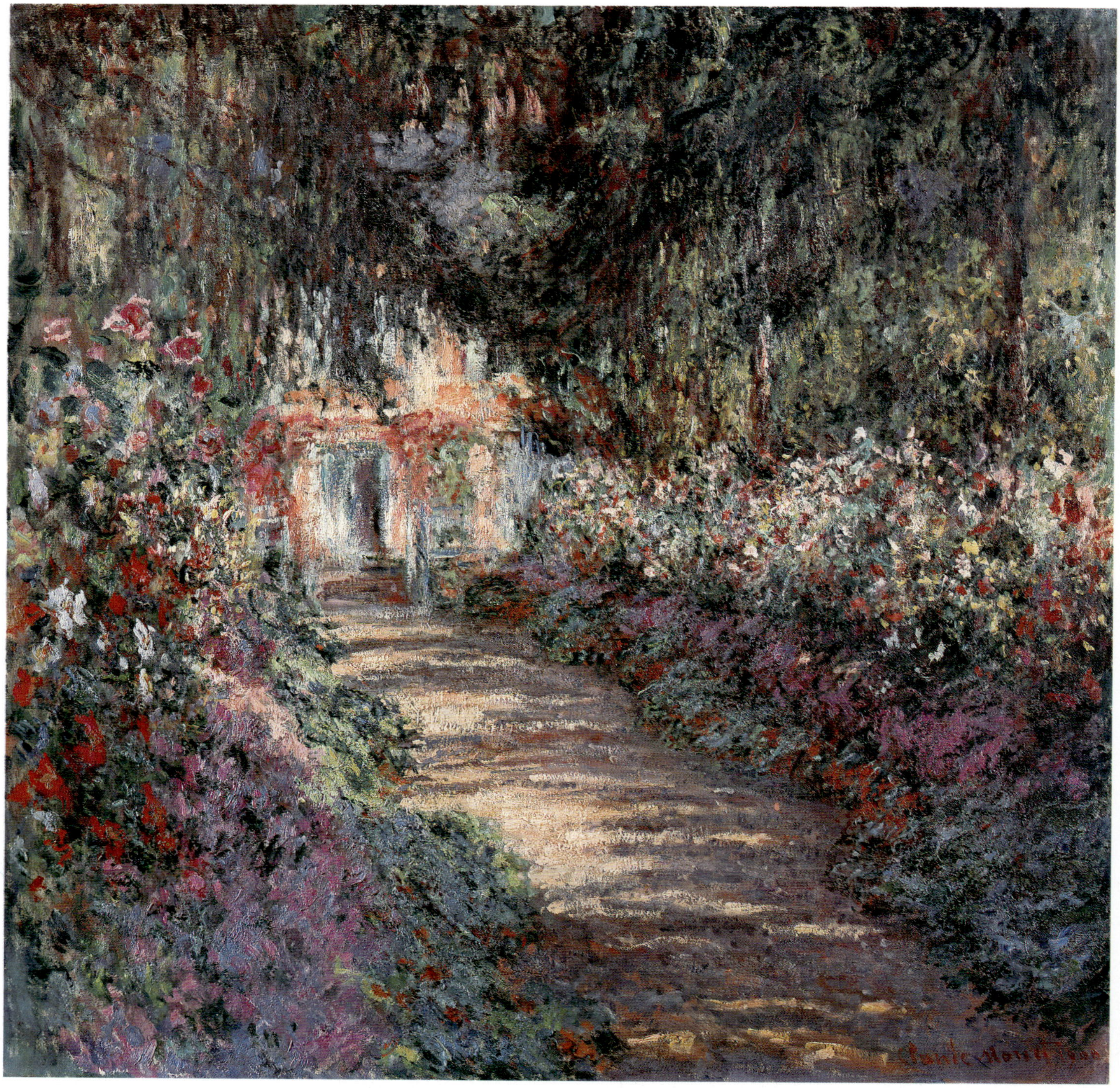

THE GARDEN IN FLOWER, 1900
Oil on canvas, 35×36¼in (89×92cm)
Private Collection

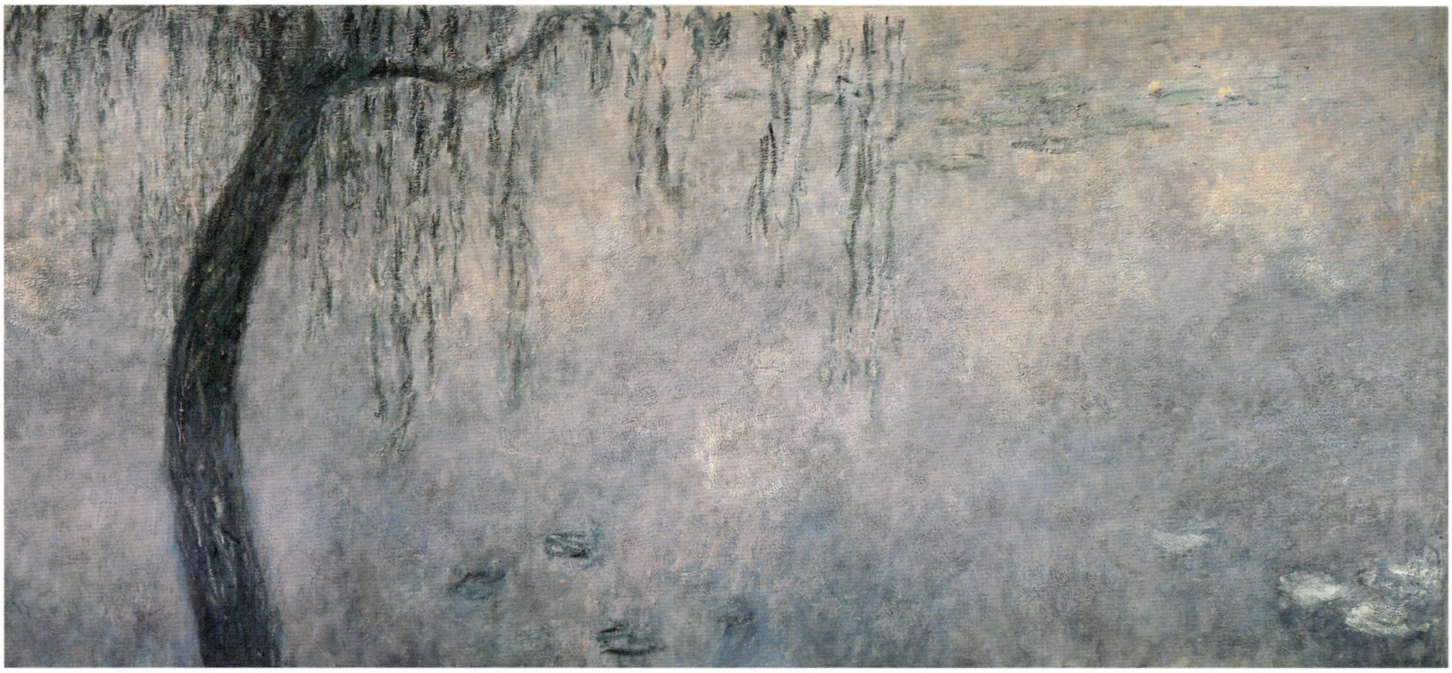

Above:
Weeping Willow, Morning Effect (detail), 1914-18
Oil on canvas, 78¼×167½in (200×425cm)
Musée de l'Orangerie, Paris

Below:
Green Reflection (detail), c. 1916-26
Oil on canvas, 78¾×335in (200×850cm) whole width
Musée de l'Orangerie, Paris

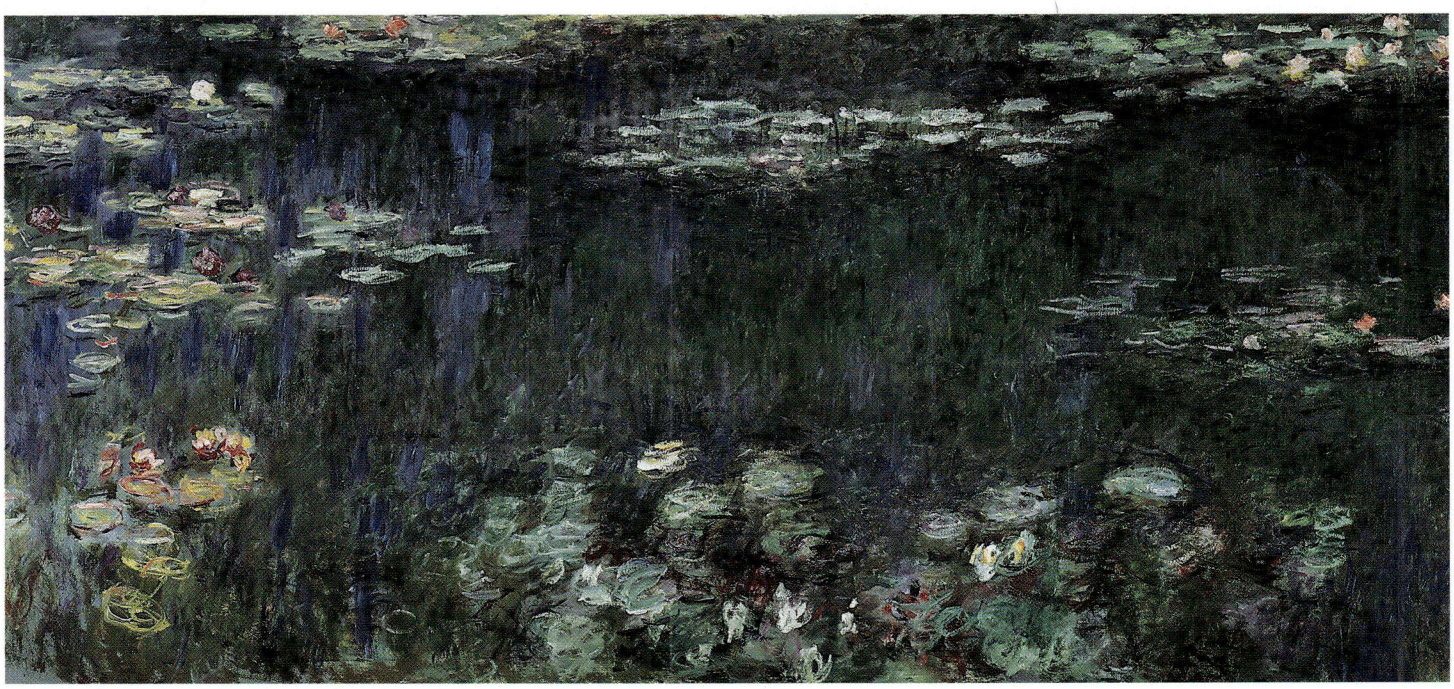

ACKNOWLEDGMENTS

The publisher would like to thank Martin Bristow who designed this book and the following institutions and individuals for supplying the illustrations:

The Art Institute of Chicago: page 18 (Potter Palmer Collection)
Kimbell Art Museum, Fort Worth, Texas: page 13
Kunsthalle, Bremen: page 14
The Metropolitan Museum of Art, New York: pages 32, 33 (Bequest of Lillie P Bliss, 1931)
Musée Marmottan, Paris: pages 24, 37, 38
Musée de l'Orangerie, Paris: page 43 (both)
Musée d'Orsay, Paris: pages 9, 15, 17, 21, 22, 26, 30
Museum of Fine Arts, Boston: pages 34 (Bequest of Robert J Edwards and Gift of Hannah Mary Edwards and Grace M Edwards in memory of their mother), 35 (Julia Cheney Edwards Collection), 36
National Gallery, London: pages 20, 40
National Gallery of Art, Washington DC: page 29 (Collection of Mr and Mrs Paul Mellon)
National Museum of Wales, Cardiff: page 39
Nelson-Atkins Museum of Art, Kansas: page 28 (Acquired through the Kenneth A and Helen F Spencer Foundation Acquisition Fund)
The Ordrupgaard Collection, Copenhagen: page 12
Private Collection: page 42
Pushkin Museum, Moscow: page 109
Städelsches Kunstinstitut, Frankfurt: page 16